D0290576

THOUGHTS WHILE TENDING SHEEP

THOUGHTS WHILE TENDING SHEEP

W.G. Ilefeldt

Woodcut illustrations by Lars Hokanson

CROWN PUBLISHERS, INC. • NEW YORK

Published by Crown Publishers, Inc., 225 Park Avenue South, New York, New York 10003 and represented in Canada by the Canadian MANDA Group

CROWN is a trademark of Crown Publishers, Inc.

Manufactured in the United States of America

Library of Congress Cataloging-in-Publication Data
Ilefeldt. W. G. (Willard G.)
Thoughts while tending sheep/W. G. Ilefeldt.
p. cm.
1. Ilefeldt, W. G. (Willard G.) 2. Shepherds—California—Biography. I. Title.
SF375.32.I44A3 1988
920.71—dc19 88-351
ISBN 0-517-56919-1

Book design by June Marie Bennett

10 9 8 7 6 5 4 3 2 1

First Edition

To my mother

CONTENTS

THOUGHTS WHILE TENDING SHEEP

And every shepherd tells his tale.
—Milton, "L'Allegro"

THOUGHTS IN ALL SEASONS

Someone once said that we are a nation of potted plants; we carry our roots around with us. Yet, some are as rootless as duckweed: a tiny, flowerlike plant, individually perfect, no more than a sixteenth of an inch in diameter, that floats on top of the water and proliferates so rapidly it took only a week for it to cover our stock pond. Apparently, its survival is dependent on its rootlessness. It is usually transported on the breasts of ducks, hence its name.

Others, however,

cannot live like that; we must put down our roots in order to survive. That is why my wife and I now live where we do, atop the Tularcitos Ridge overlooking the Carmel and Cachagua valleys.

We moved here from the city when I retired and now raise between twenty and thirty sheep. If I chose to raise more, it would require more land. Consequently, for six months of the year I am forced to be a shepherd for a couple of hours twice a day, rain or shine.

We have seven fenced-in pastures, but if my neighbors did not let my sheep graze on their land the sheep would eat up all our grass, leaving none for the summer when we have no rain. Even so, to get them through the summer I have to haul in six tons of alfalfa and a couple of tons of grain.

I have a sheepdog, a Border collie by the name of Maxine. I call her Maxie. She is a little over three years old. I have had her about a year. She was trained to do what she does and she does it very well: sometimes too well, herding them when they should be left alone to graze, reminding me of people who would want to fix the break of day. She was named and trained by someone else, but she responds to my commands most of the time, even though I suspect she thinks she knows more about sheep than I do. Perhaps she does. Not only is she smart, but she is the most loyal and loving dog I have ever had.

While I am out shepherding, there is not much else for me to do except lean against a tree and occasionally send Maxie out to fetch a sheep that has strayed a little too far from the flock. Before I got her I had to fetch the strays myself. Therefore, with Maxie eager to work, leaving me with all this time on my hands, I think a lot.

IN THE DARK HIDDEN PLACES DANGER LURKS

The north slope of our ridge is densely wooded. The front of our house faces north. The land to the south and west, where the pond, the barn, and the fenced-in pastures are, is level with the house. Immediately below the house is another level area of several acres. Beyond it the ground slopes down to level off every several hundred feet and halts the abrupt fall of the land.

During the summer, when the foliage is thick, we

cannot see beyond the first stand of trees. But after the leaves have fallen, leaving only a few live oaks and bays in full dress, only then can we see through the scrim of empty branches to the valley below. It is then that we also catch glints of vivid color that are otherwise hidden behind the leaves: toyons laden with clusters of red berries and an occasional madrone, whose blistered outer skin has peeled back to reveal its sunburned trunk.

Back east, winter means snow and spring brings rain and new growth, but here rain comes only in the winter. It is then that our grass turns green.

Several years ago I fenced in the area below us and, as I have since removed most of the dead trees and fallen limbs for firewood, the sun filters through to make the grass grow more abundantly than before. Thus, when I cannot take the time to graze the sheep out in the open, I turn them loose in the lower acreage where they can graze without me and Maxie to tend them.

After the first year, the sheep cleared the whole area of brush and low-hanging branches, leaving the floor of this once-wild forest looking like a well-kept parkland. I also bulldozed a trail to circle down into this lower area, and since the grass had grown back, and the sheep keep it nicely mown, it makes a lovely woodland pathway for my wife,

Louise, and me to walk down at a peaceful and leisurely pace. (Nature has a way of healing some of the wounds we inflict upon it.) But farther down the slope, in the dark hidden places that remain, danger lurks.

The first year we moved in, Louise and I were eating breakfast in the dining room that overlooks the level area immediately below us. I saw something stir. It was so well camouflaged I would not have seen it had it not moved. I told Louise where to look, but by this time the creature had become still. It was only after it moved again that Louise saw it too. It was a huge mountain lion. We watched it until it got up and slowly disappeared down the slope. The next morning it was in the same spot again.

Shortly thereafter, I began removing a few trees to open more of the area to the sun and topped a number of the larger oaks so that from our deck we could see over them and catch a glimpse of the Monterey Bay far to the northwest. This left nowhere on the level for the lion to hide in and spring out from to kill an unsuspecting deer as one chanced by. We never saw it there again.

Some would say I had no business denying the lion its right to the hidden shadows from which it could make its living. There are probably just as many who are equally concerned about the plight of the defenseless deer on which such predators feed.

I had always shared these concerns with typical sentimental deference to weaker creatures until I heard an account told by a forest ranger about twenty-five years ago when my family and I were camping in Colorado near the rim of the Grand Canyon. He said that a few years before a group of concerned folks got together and petitioned the authorities to eliminate predators, which have an unfair advantage over deer and other defenseless prey. They made their appeal so emotional and convincing that the authorities had to accede to their demand and hire professional hunters to kill the predators off. According to him, they did such a good job of it that the deer population grew to an extent that they overgrazed the grasslands, and more of them died of starvation than would have been killed had no action been taken. It was years before the balance of nature was restored.

This story changed my thinking. Even when I decided to raise sheep I clung to the conclusion that predators have as much right to live as do the defenseless creatures on which they prey. It was up to me to keep my sheep out of harm's way. But last year I lost three lambs.

The killing of certain tiny, defenseless creatures generally makes us angry. It makes us want to get back at that which has caused us to experience the mental pictures we have of the innocent victim's horrible suffering and death.

The more I thought about it, the more I realized that the rage I felt was little different from when I instinctively slap in anger at an insect that has bitten me. More to the point: Most of us think nothing of setting a mousetrap or taking a swatter to a fly. An insect is hardly a predator; it is merely a pesky annoyance to most of us, unless, of course, it is a mosquito that carries malaria, a flea that spreads typhoid fever, or a wasp whose sting causes a life-threatening allergic reaction in some people. I have concluded, therefore, that our concern for defenseless prey tends to be selective. It has more to do with the victim's size, or certain qualities of endearment that invite our sympathy, than it does with logic.

But I must admit, I did not feel kindly toward the lion that got my lambs. I was outraged, even though reason told me it was doing what instinct and hunger compelled it to do in order to survive. Yet, I was not about to have it tracked down and killed as neighbors across the valley had done to the one that killed several of their livestock. Perhaps if my livelihood depended entirely on raising sheep I might have thought otherwise.

THE DEATH OF ACHILLES

Achilles was the first ram we got after we moved here and started raising sheep. I got him from the Wilsons, who sold him cheap because he had foundered. I asked what *foundered* meant. "He's gone lame," I was told. "He's got bad feet." That is why he was named Achilles.

Actually, it was Louise who named him. She is a great one for names. The ram we got most recently she named Studley. We call him Stud for short. She gets names from everywhere. She got the names Shirley, Goodness, and

Mercy from the Twenty-third Psalm because she said these three little lambs tended to "follow me all the days of their life." One of the little rams she named Agnus Dei, which we later changed to Angus Day because most of our pagan friends thought that was what we meant anyway but were pronouncing it with a phoney Scotch accent.

The Wilsons could not sell Achilles on the regular market because he could not make it on the open range. But they assured me he would be ideal on a smaller ranch like ours. If Achilles had not gone lame he would have brought a top price as a prize ram. Despite his bad feet, the rest of him functioned well enough for him to settle the ewes, who have a way of slowing down when a ram cannot quite keep up.

Achilles did his job well, siring many fine sheep. They all turned out so well that three years ago I decided to keep five of his daughters from that year's crop of lambs and start another flock. I could not use Achilles as the sire of this new flock, however, as it would weaken the offspring, so I bought another ram. I got it from a local 4-H'er. It had come in second at the Monterey Fair and had good bloodlines. Louise named it Avis.

When the rainy season starts and the grass is tall enough, I usually run the two flocks of impregnated ewes in together and take them out to graze in the open, reserving one of the fenced-in pastures to put the two rams in.

Once the rams determine which one is to dominate the other, they tend to live in peace with each other. The first year Achilles dominated Avis, probably because he was older. But the next year Avis dominated Achilles. His poor feet gave the younger one the advantage. The heads of both rams were bleeding from where they had butted each other in order to find out which was the stronger. But Achilles survived and took his position as second best with the proud nobility of a former champion.

I was intent on upgrading the flock and the next year I sold Avis and replaced him with a more expensive ram. It was the one Louise named Studley. He was a superb beast, had good feet and all the good features you look for in a ram. My experience in such matters was paying off.

In late spring I turned the two rams in with the ewes, each with his own harem. And this fall, as I usually do, I joined the two flocks of ewes and put Achilles in a separate pasture with Stud. The expected battle ensued. Achilles got whipped. This too was expected, but poor Achilles was so badly beaten he refused to eat and drink. His brain must have become addled from the butting Studley gave him. The next morning, when I discovered what had happened and thinking that Stud was also preventing Achilles from the feeding area, I separated them. But nothing helped. Achilles was so badly beaten he remained in a deep depression. Yesterday, Achilles died. I buried him today.

♦

"Things That Go Bump in the Night"

While I was digging his grave I found myself thinking about death and how my grandmother dealt with it. She had a way about her that made us kids want to believe in a world that is beyond the real world. She did not consider it spooky or in any way frightening. She just made the world we live in the enchanting place it is because there was this other world too. The fact that no one could prove or disprove that this other world did or did not exist did not keep us from believing in it. She always acted as if it did and behaved accordingly. We did too.

People who have lost a leg claim they can still feel sensations in it long after it is amputated. They complain of it itching or of its feeling numb. The medical profession calls this a "phantom limb." This phenomenon had been suggested as the possible reason the American Indian does not consider the soul of the departed ready for the next world until all the body of the deceased is assembled in the same place. Which, of course, conjures up all sorts of speculation about restless spirits searching about for parts they are missing, accounting for those "things that go bump in the night," haunting old houses.

Skeptics would dismiss such manifestations as illusionary. But my grandmother would not go along with that. For example, she claimed that several days after my grandfather died and was buried she saw him "appear," walking up the stairs of their home. According to her, there was nothing frightening about his appearance. It seemed to comfort her. And whatever comforted her tended to comfort us.

There are those who would claim that this so-called appearance was caused by her bereaved mind finding a way of coping with grief. This would seem a plausible explanation for some people, but for her, "seeing grandpa" in this way merely strengthened her belief in the reality of the spirit world, a world beyond the living. It enhanced her faith in the distinct probability of joining him in an afterlife that was promised to her by her religious faith. For her, it eased the terror of death and made less likely an everlasting separation from the ones she loved.

♦

First-Time Mothers

After I lost the lambs to the predator, and thinking of ways of preventing these kills from happening again, I made an interesting discovery: The three lambs I lost were the offspring of ewes who were mothers for the first time. How could this be, I asked myself, when first-time mothers are usually overprotective of their lambs and defend them when they are in danger of attack?

I began watching the behavior of all my ewes toward their lambs and concluded the following: The first rule of nature is, a mother's needs are primary, otherwise the little ones who are dependent on her for nurture will not survive on their own. Unfortunately, some first-time mothers are so intent on observing the first rule—feeding themselves—that after a week outside the lambing pen they sometimes forget their young. While she is grazing she will let one of her twins wander off, apparently satisfied that as long as one is nearby the other is following along too. She becomes so preoccupied with feeding herself she does not realize that one of her lambs, probably exhausted from trying to find her, is now sleeping under a tree over on the next hill. When she discovers her lamb missing, she races off in search of it, leaving the other to fend for itself. This behavior led me to believe it was no mere coincidence that first-time mothers let their lambs get lost more often than experienced mothers.

Lambs are born, nursed, weaned, and in a matter of months are ready for market. A good breed ewe will correct mistakes and do better the next year. But among humans, a normal reproductive and nurturing life cycle takes about twenty or more years. A generation. By the time a human mother has experienced all the difficulties of raising her young, and supposedly has learned thereby, her rearing years are over. She has no chance to correct her mistakes the way a sheep does.

As I look back on what happened to me, when I was a kid, I wonder if some of my mother's decisions would be judged good ones. You decide.

MY DEBUT

The things we remember from early childhood are often remembered only because we have heard them from some adult who was there at the time and tells us about it. I do not consider that remembering. Photographs do the same thing. For instance, there is a snapshot in an old album of me seated inside an open valise holding a little white dog in my arms. The valise was about the size of the leather bag doctors used to carry with them when they made house calls, which gives an idea of how long ago that was and how small I was at the time.

I mention the snapshot only because I do not remember the dog or who took the picture. It was probably my father. He was always doing funny things, so I am told. I have to rely on the word of others because he was not around long enough for me to remember him.

Mother once told me about a concert he was giving somewhere in Texas. It was probably Dallas or Fort Worth. She was in the audience while I was left in the care of a black woman, a kind of live-in baby-sitter who also accompanied us when we traveled. I do not remember her name for I was only two and a half at the time and there is no one left to tell me.

Thinking I was safely asleep in my father's dressing room, my baby-sitter left me to go to the wings to hear him sing. Somehow, I managed to slip by her, right out onto the stage, and stood next to him while he was in the middle of a song. You can imagine the audience's response, to say nothing of the distress my mother must have felt. I just stood there beside him and, as though it were the most natural thing to do, he reached down and held my hand until the song was over, then led me offstage and back into the care of a very stricken and self-chastised baby-sitter.

My father returned for the applause, which was probably greater than it would have been had I not appeared and had he not carried it off so well.

The applause continued. It was obvious they wanted me. Showman that my father was, he carried me back onstage. We got an ovation. But to show how unreliable one's memory of childhood events are, I do not remember a thing about it.

There are two events I do remember, though, that I know were not told me by someone else. The first—if it was the first—was the day I accompanied my father to his workshop, which was separate from the house. He was good with tools and enjoyed making things when he was not leading band practice, giving singing lessons, or out of town giving a concert. (I still have a pair of brass candlesticks he made.)

The mental picture I have of the workshop is hazy, but I do remember wearing a child's suit with a loose belt around it. There were some wooden blocks lying around on the floor I wanted to take home and play with, but the suit I wore had no pockets, so we tucked the blocks under the belt and tightened it. My father then picked me up and carried me home on his shoulders with my legs around his neck. I wonder why I remember something as simple as that and do not remember walking out onstage and standing beside him in front of all those people.

The only other thing I remember about him has to do

with his taking me to the circus. Mother was not with us for some reason. She was pregnant with my sister and did not accompany us, or perhaps she was doing some shopping while my father and I were outside talking to some men who recognized him. I do not remember a thing about the circus itself, even the clowns, the trapeze artists, or the wild animals. Apparently, the behavior of my father was much more memorable. Here he was, a man well known and respected, on a busy streetcorner, demonstrating how the elephants at the circus rolled over on their sides. He actually got down on the sidewalk and rolled over. The men were laughing. I was laughing too. He could make people laugh. It was as though his whole purpose in life was to entertain.

Those two events are the only things I remember firsthand about my father, except for his funeral. I do not remember the circumstances of his dying. Things like that are kept from children. But I do remember sitting with my mother in chairs next to the grave while the service was going on. We were the only ones sitting down. All the rest—and there were many who came to pay their respects—were standing. Like all children that age I did not understand the meaning of death. My father was often away giving concerts. Therefore, his absences were no big thing for me, for he always came back. But I do remember crying. I was crying because my mother was crying. I had never seen her do that before.

To show how sudden and unexpected his death was, he died just a week after he gave the concert at which I walked out onstage and stood beside him. A couple of months later my sister was born. I was not able to remember my father any better than she did, except for those two events I told about.

♦

Another Charlie Chaplin

Now, everyone who knew my father and told me about him later said he was a very funny man. He had a serious side too, but I rarely heard much about that side of him. It was as if people wanted to remember only his fun side. He was respected professionally, and everyone said he might have become famous had he not died so young. And there may be no direct connection to what later killed him, but he got laryngitis every winter during the height of the opera and concert season, which, they said, was what held back his career as a performer. In order for him to sing with any reliability he was forced to leave Boston, where he grew up, and go to a climate warmer than Boston, New York, Philadelphia, or Chicago. His brother Fritz was a violinist for the Dallas Symphony and suggested he come and make his living in Texas. "They're eager for culture down here, and they have more money from raising cattle and pumping oil than they know what to do with," he had written.

My parents were married in 1913 and moved to Texas soon after. I was born in 1917, and two and a half years later my father died at the age of thirty-seven of diabetes. (Thirty-seven was probably about the average lifespan of a diabetic in those days. A couple of years later insulin was isolated and doctors started prescribing it to prolong the lives of those who had the disease.) He and everyone else considered him a vigorous and healthy man. His behavior as a jolly man, and ever the performer, along with his enormous size and energy—he weighed two hundred and thirty-five pounds—hid the disease that was to kill him.

To give an idea of what a funny man he was, Mother told the following story. In Boston, where my mother also grew up, in the early 1900s, people got from one place to another by electric streetcar or by carriage. There were few autos then because automobiles were for rich people. My father was not rich when he was courting her. The rapid transit system that ran through Boston had streetcars with benches that ran along each side of the car. Passengers on one side sat facing those on the other side of the aisle. When it was crowded, those who stood had to hang on to straps that hung from the ceiling.

My father was escorting my mother to the opera. He was not performing that night, but in those days it was not uncommon for men to wear a dinner jacket or tails to the opera, so it was not the elegant way he was dressed that caused the other passengers to notice him.

The car was not crowded, and after they sat down he tried to cross his legs. Because he was about the size of Pavarotti he could not, or he made it look like he failed. But he persisted and finally succeeded in getting his right foot up on his left knee and kept it there by holding on to his pants leg. By then he had attracted the attention of all the passengers. All the while my mother was trying to act as if he belonged to someone else. And just as he succeeded in getting his foot on his knee and everyone began to relax, he released his grip on his pants leg and his foot slipped off.

Undaunted, he began the whole process again, and after he had done this several times, only to have his foot slip back down, he had his audience convulsed. He did not let on he was trying to be funny. To them he represented everyman in his endless struggle to overcome the insurmountable, always to fail. They were on his side because he never gave up trying, and they laughed because he retained his dignity throughout as all good clowns do. And he did it without a clown's grotesque makeup: What could be more elegant than he and his pretty lady companion dressed in evening clothes? They laughed because he was making fun of pretention, as Chaplin was to do in films in which he played the elegantly dressed little tramp. But my father did not live long enough to make it to Hollywood and fame.

◆

"To Grandmother's House We Go"

When my father died in the early twenties, there was no such thing as welfare as we know it today. There were the Poor House, the Old Folks House, the Orphanage, but no Aid to Families with Dependent Children, food stamps, or surplus cheese. My mother had to go to work or return to Boston.

She was not about to live off her parents. With no training except housekeeping, the best situation she could find was a job as a housemother for a dormitory of boys in the

Texas State Orphan's Home in Corsicana. She became a substitute mother for about twenty boys, aged five to twelve. Her duties were to see that they made their beds, took their showers, got to meals and classes on time, and behaved themselves. She also ordered their clothing and saw that they were dressed presentably. They would have done anything for her; they adored her.

After working at the home for five years, she was finally persuaded to move back to Boston. Her parents had been after her to do that all along, but she had reasons of her own for not wanting to. She was an independent person and the best example of any woman I have ever known who managed to make a good living without making a big thing out of it. She just did what needed to be done, and I never heard her complain about how life had treated her, or how unfair the world was to a widow who had to make it in a workplace that favored men. She never made as much as men who did the same kind of work. She was so busy earning enough for us to survive on that it never occurred to her to fight for equal pay. It just was not done in those days. She probably would have lost her job if she had.

Ostensibly we were to go to Boston during the summer of 1925 for a visit only. My sister and I were told we would probably return to the Home in the fall, but I noticed

Mother packed all our things in several trunks. She explained that they were to be shipped to Boston only if she decided we were to stay permanently. It is true she did not want to be a burden on her parents, and jobs were difficult to get for a woman without skills, but there were other reasons I was unaware of at the time that made her hesitate about leaving Texas.

My grandparents' house was huge. There had been seven children, all of whom had married and were living elsewhere when we got to Boston. Four bedrooms were on the second floor and three in the "attic." But there was only one bathroom in the whole house. There was, however, a single toilet down in the cellar where the furnace and laundry sinks were. The use of the one bathroom must have been a source of constant frustration and called for the utmost forbearance on the part of all members of my mother's family. There was at least one mandatory bath to be taken on Saturday night by each of the children in preparation for church the next day. "Whether you need it or not," my grandmother used to tell the boys.

Hot water was, of course, limited, so the same bathwater was used for several of the children. The cleanest went first. I can understand why all my mother's brothers and sisters married young.

After they all left home, there were all these rooms going to waste. Therefore, my grandmother began taking in boarders, most of whom were men with families back in Germany. None of them ever complained about the one bathroom because it was one more than they had back home. Most of them stayed no longer than a couple of years, until their families could join them, or until the single men got settled enough in their jobs (or saved enough) to get married to a woman they met here and make a home for themselves.

My grandfather was away most of the time. After he retired he was skipper of James J. Storrow's yacht, which was moored near where the Storrow Drive now runs along the Charles River. I never saw it, but I was told the yacht had a crew of five, so it must have been a big one.

Before his "retirement," my grandfather had captained merchant vessels between Boston and Europe. He met my grandmother for the first time when his ship rescued all the passengers on hers before it went down. Years later, when one of the Boston newspapers ran a human interest story on their fiftieth wedding anniversary, it said he was the captain of the boat that rescued her. He was only second in command, but the reporter must have thought it more romantic to give him a promotion. I noticed no one ever demanded a retraction.

I never got to know my grandfather well. It is just as well because he was a man of the old school; he believed in discipline. It was around that time when just about everyone thought discipline was exactly what I needed. Grandpa had been in the German Imperial Navy before going into merchant shipping. My grandmother may have thought him handsome and romantic, but he was too strict for me. He had a Kaiser Wilhelm mustache, which gives an idea of how he thought of himself. Others may have thought him impressive-looking, but he always looked stern to me. He frightened me. I never felt he liked me, probably because I had trouble keeping still. I was into everything, and did not obey commands readily. I had a problem.

Even if I overheard the grown-ups discussing it at the time I do not remember. I was having too good a time to pay much attention to what they were worried about. But during the summer of 1925 my mother was looking for a job. She finally found one with a dentist, the kind that straightens children's teeth, which in those days was in its experimental stage and was probably pretty primitive compared to today's techniques.

That first year, while she was learning her job, Mother must have been paid very little, barely enough to support herself even if she lived with my grandparents, but she was to stay in that job for the next thirty years. In those days only men did the kind of work she did and, because she was a woman, she was paid far less than they. All things considered, that was probably the only reason she got the job in the first place and was able to hold on to it for so long. Although she did not receive wages equal to them, she earned much more than most men earned during the Depression, which came shortly after we moved from Texas.

It was later I was to understand why my mother hesitated about leaving Texas. It was because she feared what might happen to my sister and me. They must have been considering separating us all along; without our knowing about it, it was decided that my sister would live with my mother's oldest brother, Otto, and his wife, Carrie. (They had lost their twelve-year-old boy to pneumonia a couple of years before. He had been an only child, and they could have no more.) It was also decided that I would live with Aunt Bertha and her husband, Bill. (It seems that Bertha kept miscarrying every time she got pregnant and, it was thought, could never bring her pregnancies to full term.) And seeing how I needed discipline (if anyone ever did!), and how Bill was supposed to be good at that, having been an officer in the Navy during the First World War, it all seemed like an ideal arrangement to everyone except me.

Mother had sent them photographs of my sister and me. I was told that when Uncle Bill saw my picture he burst out laughing and said he had always wanted a boy who looked just like me. I look at that picture now and I can see why he laughed. I must have been one of the funniest-looking kids you ever saw. Just before the picture was taken I was told to comb my hair. I used water to wet the comb, and about an inch of my hair stood straight up in front while the rest lay flat. I had a cowlick (I still do). I also had freckles. I had this big grin on my face that reached from ear to ear. In other words, I was not what you would call handsome, but, apparently, I was someone Uncle Bill wanted.

I know some folks would blame my mother for allowing my sister and me to be separated from each other and from her, but she was under a lot of pressure with everyone telling her that what I needed was discipline, the firm kind that only a man like Uncle Bill could give. Today, they would say I needed a male image, a father figure. I suppose that was part of what I needed, but I also needed my mother, because it was just about then that everything seemed to go wrong.

THE DUMB KID

Usually, when a sheep has a normal birth, it all seems so effortless. But when the baby lamb is placed wrong, you have to give help or the little one will not make it. Even worse, the ewe will not either. You have to reach in and turn the lamb around so its front legs and nose present themselves first.

Assisting a difficult birth for the first time can be pretty traumatic. But now that I have had to do it about three or four times, confident enough to handle any problem—even a human birth if I had to, like some taxi drivers you read about who cannot get the mother to the hospital on time. It is easy, except when there is a prolapse. That is when the ewe gives birth to its uterus along with the lamb. There is not much you can do once that happens, except push it all back in. So far, I have not had any success with that kind of problem. By the time the vet gets here—if he will agree to come this far out—the ewe has already died of exhaustion and shock, or whatever. Now, I just shoot her to put her out of her misery. Mine too.

And after all these years, I have gotten pretty good at telling when a ewe is about to give birth. When she starts to isolate herself from the flock, looking off into the distance for a place to be alone, and holding back when it is time for me to take them out to graze, I know a birth is going to happen in the next couple of hours. But before it does, I put her in a lambing pen with enough water and feed to sustain her, and leave her alone to have her lamb on her own. I check up on her every half hour or so and, if it looks like it is going to be a difficult birth, I stay with her and help any way I can. Usually it is not necessary. But sometimes I am not around when the birthing process starts. That can be a problem if she is having trouble.

A couple of years ago, for example, Fudge, my oldest and best ewe, started labor during the night. The next morning, when the sheep were waiting for me to take them out to graze, I noticed Fudge missing. I went looking for her and found her under a tree. Overnight she had given birth to twins, one of which was stillborn. She had labored during the long night and, in the process, the umbilical cord, which supplies the lamb with life-giving oxygen until it is born and can breathe on its own, had been pinched off while the lamb was still in the birth canal struggling to be born. The other lamb was alive. Just barely. When it tried to get up and nurse it had trouble standing. I picked it up by its front feet, holding it down near the ground at arm's length, and walked toward the lambing pen with Fudge following after her lamb. I then left the two of them together to get acquainted while I went back and dug a grave for the stillborn. When I got back to the lambing pen I noticed the little lamb was still wobbly on its feet. Usually, newborn lambs will be that way for the first hour or so, but this one was still too unsteady on its feet to be normal. It, too, I concluded, had been placed wrong, and whereas its twin had died because of a lack of oxygen, this one had survived but was left brain-damaged.

In all other respects this little lamb was well formed and

perfect. Handsome, in fact. All of Fudge's lambs are. But this one walked funny. Later, when I took them out with the flock to graze, it was even more obvious something was wrong. It managed to keep up with the rest of them, but it had the kind of abnormality that is a clear signal to predators. A predator, it seems, is not interested in the sport of the kill. It is hungry, and will take any advantage, always seeking out the lame, the sickly, and the unalert, in order to get a meal in the easiest way possible. It will attack only when it has a better-than-even chance of success, knowing that when the prey is healthy, fleet of foot, and always on the alert, it will escape nine times out of ten. Experts tell us it is nature's way of improving the species so that only the fittest survive.

But I was not about to give up on this one. It was in no pain and, apparently, was unaware it was any different from the others. It had as good a life as any of the other lambs, always gamboling around the way little lambs do when they feel exuberant and frisky.

Little lambs are amusing when they bounce around on all fours, prancing on tiptoe, but this one was downright funny; it could never get its hind end coordinated with its front end when it covorted around with the other lambs celebrating life. It would be a mistake to keep him for breeding purposes; I never could be sure he could get his hind end to do what needed to be done.

One time, walking along with the rest of the flock near the edge of the pond, it fell, or was crowded, off the embankment into the water. I heard it bleat in distress. It began swimming around in circles, and every time it would baa it would get a mouthful of water, which made its cry even more agonizing. It would try to swim back to the embankment to climb ashore, but when it could not find footing it baaed and swam back out again.

From the shore I tried to scare it across the pond, where it could touch ground and wade ashore where it was shallower, but I stopped short of going in after it, it being January. I sent Maxie in instead.

With Maxie swimming in pursuit, the little guy finally got to the opposite side, apparently unharmed. And once ashore it ran to find solace from Fudge, who, while all this was going on, was making an even greater racket than the lamb. After it nursed long enough to realize it was safe again, it tried to shake the water off. Usually, when a sheep shakes off water it starts at one end and works toward the other in well-coordinated spasms. But this little fellow started shaking in several places at once. It never did get it right.

Amusing though it was, I had the greatest sympathy for this little brain-damaged lamb, for I, too, had a handicap when I was a kid. I could not read. Apparently, I saw the written word reversed or inverted. This phenomenon is usually found in boys who are also hyperactive. They now have names for what was wrong with me: dyslexia and hyperkinesis. Years later we were told that Woodrow Wilson, Nelson Rockefeller, and Albert Einstein, among other famous people, had had the same problem. But had I known I was included with such illustrious company, it would not have eased the discomfort I felt about myself. Back then I was just a "dumb kid."

♦

God Is Love

Even kids who I knew were dumber than I were reading before I could. I was not good at figures either. The only thing I was good at was music. I could carry a tune. I took after my father. Perfect pitch, they said. I could not read music any better than I could read words, but when we sang in school and church, I could follow what the rest were singing, because in no time at all I became familiar with the words and music. It was then I could really let loose. When that is about the only thing you've got going for you, you make the best of it.

But that was indoors. Outdoors I was good at sports. I could run faster than any kid my age, even faster than most of the older kids, which made up for not being able to read. Almost.

But then there was the radio. If you cannot read you can always listen to the news, drama, and music. But the kind of love you heard about on radio was different from the kind you heard about in church. The kind they were always singing about in popular songs was supposed to make us kids snicker. I did not know why then. Knowledge about that kind of love was something you grew into, like when you got old enough to smoke and you got a driver's license, when everything was supposed to become clear.

Church was different from school. That was where it made no difference if you could read or not because all the stories from the Bible were told to us. And they were wonderful stories. I loved them. I identified, as I suppose all children do, with these mighty heroes who could do magical things, like Moses parting the Red Sea, David and Goliath, Daniel in the lion's den, and Shadrach, Meshach, and Abednego. I was fascinated and daydreamed about them all week and could not wait until the next Sunday to hear more of these astounding stories.

In church we were told that God is love. It seems that God's kind of love was the kind you had toward members of your family. You were supposed to take it more seriously than the romantic kind. You did not have to be able to read to be able to love. Some of the time I did not understand what the preacher was talking about. It was way over my head, especially when he said we were supposed to love our enemies. Usually, I only listened when he was telling a story. It was not until years later that I understood what he meant by God's Grace. He never said so in so many words—if he had I would have understood right off—but God's Grace meant being loved even when you are a dumb kid. I was.

♦

I Loved Going to Church

To add to my problem of not being able to read, when I moved in with Bertha and Bill I started to wet the bed. Rather than anyone admitting that this nightly embarrassment may have been caused by my being separated from my mother and sister—because I had not wet the bed on a regular basis since I was around three—they came up with another reason: They said it was because I had had scarlet fever a couple of years before and it left me with weak kidneys. Recent findings suggest that bed-wetting is a tendency that runs in certain families, and it is usually boys who are more likely than girls to be victims of this inherited trait. The same is said of dyslexia and hyperkinesis. It was probably a combination of all these factors. But even if I were given all the reasons in the world that would excuse them or me from blame, it would not have made me feel any better. I may have been made to feel forgiven for being a dumb kid who could not read, but to be a bed wetter too—at the age of nine!—was unforgivable.

In the fall of 1925 I was enrolled at the Cutter School in Arlington, a town just outside of Boston. I lived with Bert and Bill in their rented second-floor flat. The Youngs, who owned the place, lived in the lower flat. They had a daughter named Errol. It was inevitable that I should fall in love with her.

Right off at school I started to get into a lot of trouble. It does not take an advanced degree in psychology to figure out why. I must have been in a fight about once a day. And every time I did I spent an hour after school in the principal's office. She was a woman principal. Teaching was about the only profession in which a woman could be in a position of authority in those days. But being an authority figure was not the only reason I considered her a threat. As a matter of fact, all adults began to act as though I was something of a problem. They might otherwise have been very nice, but I only saw their sterner side. If grown-ups think you are dumb they are likely to be forgiving, but because of the way I was behaving I was a threat to their authority. Controlling a dumb kid is easier than handling a combative one, and I was becoming more combative all the time.

If you are hyperactive, I guess having to sit still is the worst kind of punishment the principal could give. I considered it worse than a whipping, for a whipping is over in no time. Having to brood over having to sit still succeeded only in building up more resentment in me. I was becoming angrier and angrier at everyone and I did not know why.

And when you take on the world, it is not long before you meet someone who is better than you. I got into a fight with a boy who beat the tar out of me. He must have harbored more anger than I, because I got a bloody nose and a swollen jaw out of it. But a funny thing happened: For the first time I did not have to spend an hour in the principal's office. He did.

It was also about this time the principal and my teacher began to realize that being separated from my mother might have something to do with my challenging the world. After that everyone began to treat me differently. I began to give up fighting on a daily basis and fought only about once a week. But then I started to do something I later became ashamed of.

When Bert married Bill she became converted to Catholicism. I was a Protestant, so I was sent to a church in the heart of Arlington. There was this drugstore at the corner where the streetcar stopped and I got off to go across the street and down a little ways to the church. As fate—or temptation—would have it, it was the only store open on Sundays. At first, I put the quarter in the collection plate every Sunday. But then, with the drugstore right there where I got off to tempt me, I figured out that if I bought an ice cream cone and the two candy bars I could have during the week, I would still have a dime left to put in the collection plate.

But by Tuesday the candy bars were gone. Something had to give. With a cone on Sunday and *three* nickels for candy (Necco Wafers preferably) I could somehow survive through the week, because when Saturday came I was then given fifteen cents—a dime for the Saturday matinee and a nickel for a candy bar. The next day was Sunday. I loved going to church.

It was not until later I became ashamed of what I did, but at the time I did not feel a thing; I figured I had it coming to me for the way they had taken me away from my mother and sister.

"WITH TWO DOGS YOU ONLY GOT HALF A DOG"

After I got Maxie, a fellow I know who has had a lifelong experience with stock dogs said, "You got a good little workin' dog there . . . but don't get another one while you got this one. If you do, instead of havin' two, you got yourself only half a dog. And if you was to get a third one, you'd have a pack."

I knew what he meant.

When we first moved here, my daughter gave me the pick of her new litter of Australian shepherds. It was a fine little puppy. I told my daughter I was going to name the dog Verity because all I ever wanted was the truth. I do not think she thought that was funny, but she laughed anyway.

Verity had all the qualities I ever wanted in a dog, but after we had her awhile, she came into season and attracted every male dog from miles around. I never saw so many different kinds, shapes, sizes, and colors. And rather than build a fence ten feet high to keep them out—and her in—it was easier for me to get Verity fixed. But before I did, there was this one dog that came one night and just made himself at home. Verity let him eat out of her bowl. This one's mine, she seemed to say. He would not go away. There was no collar with a tag to identify him by name, whether he had had shots, or who the owner was. I advertised in the local paper trying to find out, but no one claimed him.

I asked some folks who live on the other side of the ridge in Cachagua Valley if they knew who the dog's owner was. They said they didn't, but I got the feeling they knew but were not about to tell me because the dog was part pit bull and they knew what it had been trained for and its ultimate fate.

We kept the dog. And not knowing his name (and he did not answer to any we tried—like Rex, Tip, Spot, Rover,

Roach, or Fang), we started calling him Sam. In no time he responded. Smart dog.

Sam, Verity, and I became the best of pals. They did as I commanded and accompanied me on long walks along Sky Ranch Road and through the woods.

But Sam had a mean streak. He did not take kindly to discipline. When I had to reprimand him because he did not behave, he would bare his teeth at me. Whereas Verity always obeyed and tried to behave herself, discipline brought out all the meanness that had been bred and trained into Sam. As long as I did not cross him, he was a loving dog, grateful for my having taken him in. He never fought with Verity, for he was her protector. He would have protected me too—such was his breeding.

But he had another bad trait: Every six weeks or so, he would take off on his own and be gone for about three hours. I never knew where. I assumed he went back and checked up on his former home; and because he always returned to us, I assumed he liked his home with us better. I thought I knew why.

When Verity got a little older, she began to accompany Sam on his periodic wanderings. Her tie to Sam was sometimes greater than that to me. They would be gone sometimes for half a day, but they always returned for their nightly feeding, exhausted but happy.

Surrounded by miles and miles of forest on every side, I could not follow them. But one morning, after they took off, I noticed on the slope across the valley from us cattle were running around with two tiny dots chasing them in a circle, like in a roundup. With my binoculars I could not make out if the two dots were Verity and Sam, but I suspected they were.

Now the whole idea of raising cattle is to get them as fat as you can in the shortest time possible. Not only do they bring more at the market, but fat causes marbling, which makes the meat more tender. But nothing burns fat off cows quicker than a couple of dogs having the time of their lives running them around in circles. Therefore, ranchers have a legal right to shoot any dog on sight that trespasses on their property.

I knew I had a problem and a serious one, and I tried confining them as punishment right after they returned. I hated keeping them penned up, however; it seemed unfair with all this open space to run around in. But how are you going to keep dogs from chasing after cattle, or anything else that runs away, once they get a taste of it? Some irate rancher would surely shoot them, and who could blame him. But the fence was not high enough. They jumped it. I had no choice but to take them to the SPCA, hoping they would find the dogs a home.

♦

Wounds That Will Not Go Away

Parting with these dogs was such a traumatic experience, it was another four years before I took a chance getting another one. Only this time I knew it had to be one that was properly trained by an expert, which was something I had already proven I could not do myself. I got Maxine.

Maxie is an expensive dog, pedigreed and all that, but well worth what I paid for her. She will leave the yard around the house only when she is with me. If I tell her to stay in one spot she will. She responds to voice command, does not seek fights with other dogs, and is superb with the sheep. I wish all dogs were like her.

But the property on the other side of the mountain was sold a few months ago. Our new neighbors are city folks. They did not understand that once you turn dogs loose to have a free run of the surrounding hills it can be a problem. They have five dogs.

When a ewe has just given birth, I keep her in the lambing pen until a bond has been established between her and her offspring. Until they are a couple of days old, lambs cannot keep up with the rest of the flock when I take them out in the open pastures beyond the pond. The new mother and her twins are content to stay in the grazing area that stretches along the road between it and the corral board fence that fronts our property.

The other day our neighbor's dogs got through the fence and made their way around the pond that separates the two properties and attacked the ewe and her two babies. We did not see it happen because Maxie and I were on the other side of the hill with the flock.

Every ewe will defend her young, but when there is more than one dog, one attacking from the front and another from the rear, it is more difficult for her to defend herself and her babies. With more than two dogs it is even worse. You can imagine what it's like with five.

When Maxie and I brought the flock back from grazing and we were on the hill that overlooks the pond, I heard the ewe bleating in distress. When I saw the dogs from the top of the hill, I yelled, "Go home!" They did. (I have a rather commanding voice.)

I could not see the two lambs. The mother ewe ran up the hill to where we were, thinking her lambs might be with us. She was foaming at the mouth. She could not find her lambs among the others. She raced back down the hill in search of them. I immediately cut short the grazing time, and Maxie and I herded the flock back to the barn area, closed the gate on them, and went searching for the two lambs, hoping they were hiding somewhere among the Monterey pines that surround the pond. But I could not find them. I went to the opposite hill and from there I saw something black lying on the shore of the pond about a foot from the edge. I could see that it was one of the little lambs, lying flat on its side with its legs stretched out. I ran down the hill, and when I approached it, it did not stir as lambs usually do when you get near them. As I got closer I could see that its neck was mangled. I stooped for a closer look. It lay perfectly still. The eye I could see was open, staring into nothingness, a complete blank. Then I saw it was breathing. I was afraid to move it for fear its neck was broken, but I picked it up in both hands, carefully supporting its head, and carried it back to the barn to its mother in one of the lambing pens. Even when its mother sniffed at it and identified it as one of her own, the little guy still did not move; it was still in shock.

I left them and went searching for the other. When I got to the entrance to our property, I noticed tufts of wool strewn all along the corral board fence. I could imagine the struggle that must have taken place with the ewe trying to protect her young ones while the dogs attacked her from all sides, taking nips at her, pulling off mouthfuls of fur with each bite, her thick fleece protecting her from more severe harm.

I finally located the other lamb. It was inside the fence standing huddled next to a tree. Apparently, while the dogs were attacking its mother, this little one escaped through the fence unharmed. The mother had been able to save at least one of her young ones by sacrificing her own safety. Her sacrifice was indeed great, I later discovered.

I picked the unharmed one up and carried it back to the barn and put it in with its mother. The other little one was still lying on its side, stretched out, barely breathing. I got a tube of Panalog, a kind of antibiotic salve you put on open wounds, and treated the bloody marks around its neck. I gave it a shot of Combiotic to ward off infection and then left; I had done all I could.

A little later I returned to the lambing pen. The injured lamb was still lying down, but I could see that life was gradually coming back. It was no longer in shock. It blinked when I passed my hand in front of its eye. I lifted it up and examined its neck. It was now swollen on one side, which led me to believe the worst: Its neck was broken. But it was breathing more deeply now, and I could only hope that the swelling in its neck would not stop its ability to breathe. I laid it back down in the warming sun. When I returned later, the little fellow was no longer lying on its side but belly down, resting its chin on the ground, its ears drooping.

By now it was several hours since the attack, and I noticed that when the unharmed lamb tried to nurse its mother pulled away. I examined the ewe. Her udder had been savaged by the dogs. There were no teeth marks that I could see, but when I tried to milk her she resisted, and the milk I squirted on the ground was pink. She had blood in her milk. She would not let me milk her other side. I pinned her bad side to the shed with my knee to keep her from pulling away, and filled a paper cup with her bloodied milk, and fed it to the injured lamb. I supported its chin while it gulped the milk down. It seemed to perk up immediately. I then gave the rest to the other one. It too drank hungrily. I left them.

That afternoon, after taking the other sheep out to graze, I tended to the mother ewe and her injured lamb. By now she was allowing her uninjured lamb to nurse, but only from the one side. The injured one still was not standing. Its neck could not support its head when it stood. I milked the ewe, fed the lamb out of a paper cup, and left them for the night.

The next morning the injured lamb was standing when I

got to the lambing pen, but its head drooped. I tried to get it to nurse but it was unable to. I milked the ewe again and fed the milk to the lamb. The mother's udder was swollen to twice its normal size. Her bag was pendulous, like a teardrop, and I wondered if she would have enough milk with only one side operating (and that one not too well) to get her twins through until they could eat solid food.

But each day the injured lamb improved. I no longer had to feed it out of a cup. It followed its mother around almost as though it had never been hurt. But neither of the lambs will grow as rapidly as other lambs. Nor will the mother be good anymore as a breed ewe; all subsequent offspring of hers will suffer the same stuntedness as these two because she will never nurse but from one side.

When I think about how these little lambs must have suffered, I cannot help comparing them with my own childhood problems and the emotional scars they caused me. These two little lambs were harmed as far as their growth was concerned, whereas I was harmed in other ways. I probably would have survived in any event, especially when you consider all the displaced children and orphans who have had to suffer deprivation of one sort or another over the centuries. But had it gone on any longer than that one year, I am sure it might have turned out worse than it did. I probably would have turned into a juvenile delinquent.

♦

Office Calls and the Price of Lamb Chops

After the dog attack, someone asked why I did not have my injured sheep treated by a vet. I have reasons: The first of which is that vets rarely make house calls anymore; they would rather you bring your animals (pets) into their offices, unless, of course, it is an expensive Arabian that warrants a large fee. Many vets no longer handle larger farm animals; it is not worth the bother. Sheep are considered large animals.

Consequently, those of us who raise sheep must rely on one another. We gladly swap information about the proper procedures in the treatment of injured and sick animals. For instance, my first experience with a sheep giving birth was a difficult one. I called Betty Wilson who lives across the valley. Over the phone I described what was going on. She said, "I'll be right over."

She sized up the problem immediately, asked for several things, some of which I did not have. But we made substitutes where we could. She annointed her hand with oil—

Wesson, I think it was, because I could find no mineral oil. She then reached in, turned the lamb around, and pulled it out. No problem.

But on examining the placenta she became concerned about its color. She poured several ounces of antibiotic into her cupped palm and reached back in, searching for a diseased, perhaps partially formed fetus. She could find none. She reassured me that the little lamb was a good one, and I probably would have no trouble with it. (I didn't.) She gave the ewe a shot of antibiotic and told me to give her a daily shot for the next couple of days. (I did.)

I asked what I owed her for her time and expertise. "Nothing," she said. "Just being neighborly." Some neighbor.

A couple of weeks ago, one of my newborn lambs got stepped on by its mother while they were in the lambing pen. The little guy could not bring its right foot forward to take a normal step. It dangled uselessly and dragged on the ground as it hobbled forward on its other three. I examined it for a break. It did not seem broken. Its shoulder appeared to be dislocated.

I called Betty. I described to her what was wrong. She said that neither she nor her husband, Bob, had ever put a dislocated joint back in place, but she thought you were supposed to pull the leg forward enough for the joint to pop back in. I tried it. It did not work. I figured I needed professional help. I called the vet in the village about eight miles away.

Knowing he no longer treated large animals, I told the girl on the phone who screens all the calls before letting you talk to the vet that it was a tiny lamb, a few days old, weighing about ten pounds, only about the size of a small dog.

"Wait a minute," she said. When she came back on she said, "Can you bring the lamb in by eleven this morning?" I told her I could.

The doctor examined the lamb and said he did not think it was a dislocated shoulder. "But I can't be sure unless I take an X-ray. I think the nerves have been injured. Then he added needlessly, "If it's untreated, its foot will show wear where it's dragged it along the ground."

After the X-rays were taken, the doctor said they showed no dislocation as he had first thought, and that he had given the injured shoulder an anti-inflammatory shot.

"Keep it penned up with its mother for the next few days to give the shot a chance to work. Give me a call on Thursday." (That was three days later.)

I thanked him, went to the window to pay. The girl started adding up the charges: office call, X-ray, anti-inflammatory shot, etc. It came to $62.00.

I said, "*What?*"

She looked over the bill, checked each item again with the list of services that had been performed, and recited each back to me with patient deliberateness.

I interrupted her. "I don't doubt that what you say is correct," I said, "but do you realize that when this lamb grows to market weight in about six months—if it survives, that is—all I'll get for it will be about what your charges come to?"

She made no reply. Her look showed sympathetic concern, mixed with an expression of I'm-only-doing-what-I'm-told-to-do. I paid the bill.

Come Thursday, the lamb still dragged its foot.

I was not about to call the vet, however, and report on the lamb's progress—or lack of it. I was afraid he would say the lamb needed another anti-inflammatory shot, and I would be charged an additional twenty or forty bucks. By then I figured I needed an anti-inflammatory shot as much as the lamb. A couple of weeks later the little guy was taken by the mountain lion, who was getting bolder than it had been the two previous years. Even though it is nature's way of reducing imperfection, you sometimes grow more attached to nature's mistakes than you do to the more fortunate ones.

BACK TO GRANDMA'S

One of the reasons I retired to ranching, after spending most of my adult life in the city, must have had to do with brief tastes of rural life in my youth, not only in Texas but in and around Boston as well.

Between my grandparents' home and the other side of the hill was a large pasture that was part of a dairy farm. Cows used to come right up to the back door. It has since been made into a public park.

On the Fourth of July the summer I returned to live with my mother in my grandparents' home after living with Bert and Bill during the previous year, we could walk through the pasture to the other side of the hill and watch the fireworks shot up by the fire department from the Boston Common five miles away.

I was told that during the Revolution the Continental Army could observe the British fleet from the top of Parker Hill. The house across the street from my grandparents' was where George Washington supposedly stayed while the British occupied the harbor. It may have been another of those places where people claim that "Washington slept here" only because it was built before the Revolution. Considering Parker Hill's strategic location—I could see Boston harbor from the window of my room in the attic—the claim seems valid enough, even if it probably is untrue.

I loved my grandparents' home. It had a lot of hidden places in the attic off the bedrooms under the roof where I could hear the mice playing at night when the lights were out. Interesting stuff had accumulated in those storage areas, which had doors you could enter if you bent down. With a flashlight I explored these spaces under the eaves looking for secret passages. There were none, but I discovered old magazines that someone—perhaps my grandfather—had saved. The *National Geographic* had pictures of African women with discs in their lips, which were supposed to make them more attractive to men. I found their exposed breasts much more so.

I also found an opera hat (the kind that snaps open), my grandfather's old uniform, his ceremonial sword and scabbard, an old muzzle-loader gun, and a flag.

Everyone was putting out flags in celebration of the Fourth of July. Boston was very patriotic back then—still is, I suppose—the Revolution, the Cradle of Liberty, Concord, Lexington, Bunker Hill, "One if by land, two if by sea," and all that. The only flag I had was the one in the attic. It was the ensign my grandfather had received when he left the German Imperial Navy. I asked if I could hang it from the porch balcony in celebration of Independence Day.

My grandmother had an amused look on her face when she told me no. It had been only a little over five years since the armistice was signed ending the First World War. There was no way I could understand why feelings ran high toward Germany.

But I did get to fire off firecrackers, which I do not remember doing back in Texas, probably because the Home did not allow them. Two-inch salutes were my favorites. They no longer permit them to be sold because they are considered too dangerous for kids.

When I discovered that a two-inch salute fit nicely into

the barrel of the muzzle-loader and marbles did too, I got this great idea: If I lit the firecracker first, dropped it down the barrel with the marble following it, and then held the gun up to aim at the target, I would have my very own firearm, the only kid in the neighborhood who did. They might have an American flag to display, but I had a gun.

I had been sufficiently warned about the danger of an exploding two-inch salute. It was an old gun, somewhat rusted before I cleaned it, but I could not tell about inside it. So, as a precaution, I wrapped it in an old quilt, placed it around the corner of the house, dropped a lighted firecracker down the barrel, and waited for it to go off. I inspected the gun. It was safe to use.

Until my ammunition ran out I had an exciting time of it perfecting my technique as a marksman. First, I would drop the lighted firecracker down the barrel, immediately followed by the marble. Then, before it went off, I raised the gun to my shoulder and aimed at the target, usually a tree. I could tell if it hit when the marble exploded on impact into a shower of clay dust. I got quite good at it, but because the season for firecrackers was soon over and I could purchase no more firecrackers, I had to content myself with playing soldier and sailor without ammunition.

Mostly I played sailor, wearing parts of my grandfather's

naval uniform. It is great to play war when you are young. Even when I fell over dead it did not hurt, unless I got tangled up with the sword. But even then I always got up and could fight another battle. When you are a mixed-up kid as I had become, living in a dream world, you can act out many hostilities. My grandmother, and her availability, also helped. She was always there when I needed her.

♦

"Not a Sparrow Falls"

After spending that year in Arlington with Bert and Bill, somewhere along the line they all must have gotten together and figured out that it was better for me to live with my mother in my grandparents' home in Boston.

Things started getting better for me right off. I was not cured of everything that ailed me; I still had a long way to go. Mother had to work, but just knowing she would be home every night gave me the security I needed. I did not wet the bed as frequently, and having my grandmother to talk to after school probably contributed as much to my improvement as anything. Everyone should have a grandmother like her when he or she is growing up. But sometimes, under the best of circumstances, things can turn out wrong. It is even worse when there is little you can do about it.

What I am referring to specifically is what happened to me and this girl I made friends with. We got on fine until one day it all ended. It had to do with a bird. We were walking through the field behind my grandparents' house when we caught sight of a bird on the ground up ahead. As we approached it, it did not fly away as we expected it would. It just moved away from us, dragging a wing.

I felt sorry for it and wanted to take it home after we caught it, feed it, wrap its wing in a splint, and make a pet of it until it mended. And then maybe I would turn it loose if it really wanted to leave. I was hoping it would not. But if it did, surely, I thought, it would return year after year with its mate in order to acknowledge its everlasting gratitude to me, the one who had restored it to health and given it its freedom. The only trouble was, the bird could not know I had all these good thoughts about what I intended doing for it.

As we got nearer, it got frightened and started scurrying around on the ground, this way and that, with the two of us scampering around trying to capture it. I told her to head it off, and when she did it darted under my foot, and all life was crushed out of it in that one abrupt moment of fate.

Now, I really liked this girl. She was about the only friend I had made up until then. But there were times when I hated her too. This was one of them.

"You killed it," she shouted.

I was speechless. Devastated. No anguish was ever so sharp in my young life. I threw myself to my knees and picked up the flattened bird and held its still warm body in my hand.

"I hate you!" she yelled. And, as if that were not enough she had to go and add: "God will hate you!" which was more than I could take. I got up and hit her. Hard.

She looked at me in disbelief. Then she turned and went off to her home, wailing, leaving me to deal with the dead bird and this awful feeling. Killing the bird was bad enough, but I had made things even worse: Now I had lost the only friend I had because I was this new kid on the block with a funny southern accent, and school had not started yet.

I took the dead bird home to my grandmother, who was usually wise about things like this. She would know what to do.

When I came into the kitchen, she was doing whatever it is grandmothers do in kitchens. I was too concerned about the dead bird I held out to her to notice anything much that was going on around me. I could say nothing. I had reached the age when boys learn they are not supposed to cry, and it is best not to talk at times like these, otherwise you will.

"Oh, you found a dead bird," she said in a way that told me she knew how I was feeling without having to tell her.

"Yes," I said, not wanting to let on I had killed it; I was too ashamed. But she must have known by the way I acted that I had something to do with it. She tried to keep me from knowing she knew.

"What should we do with it?" she asked.

"I don't know."

"We could give it a proper burial," she suggested.

I had thought about that too, but I had also been thinking about having it stuffed like they do at the Museum of Natural History.

"Yeah," I said, realizing now that it would be better having the bird out of sight so as not to keep reminding me I had stepped on it.

Grandma became all business, giving orders. But she did it quietly, which I knew was out of respect for the bird and the way I was feeling. She told me to find her prayer book next to her bed while she looked for something to bury it in. When I brought it to her, she had already found a suitable coffin. It turned out to be a tin can my grandfather's pipe tobacco came in. It was red and had a hinged top. Any can would have done as long as it had a cover to keep the worms out, but the bird slipped into this one just fine. You could not have asked for a better fit. My grandfather smoked Prince Albert.

"Where should we bury it?" she asked.

"Out back, under the tree," I said.

I dug the hole. It did not take long; the earth was soft. It was the kind that had a lot of worms in it, so I was glad we were using a tin can instead of a cardboard box or a paper bag that would have rotted in no time at all.

Grandma became solemn when she opened her prayer book. She searched around in it until she found the right page and then said, "There isn't a burial service for birds, so we'll use the one for children, and when I come to the word 'children,' I'll say 'little ones.'"

She read some things I recognized because I had to learn them by heart in Sunday school along with the Lord's Prayer. (When you cannot read you become good at memorizing things.) Then she read some other stuff about how it would no longer be hungry or thirsty, and the sun would not burn it, and a Lamb would lead it to fountains of living water and wipe away all tears.

Finally, she put her arm around my shoulder and we said the Lord's Prayer together. Then she said, "You can bury it now." I did. After I finished, she said, "Let's go in and have some tea and cookies."

We went into the kitchen and she poured a cup of tea for herself and gave me a cup of hot water with milk and sugar in it. She called it "Cliffit's Tea." (I do not know if that is the way it is spelled, but it sounded like that.)

In those days I was always asking dumb questions. Like the time I asked my mother how long it took for an ant to fall from the water tower. Another time I asked where the light went when you turned off the switch.

"Grandma," I asked, "why do things die?"

She looked at me and said quietly, "Everything has to die."

"I know that—but why?" I persisted.

She thought about it before she answered. "I don't know; it's just the way things are."

I waited for her to go on, and when she did not I said, "It's not fair."

"No, dear, it isn't."

She said nothing for a long time. I guess she was as stumped as I was. Then she added: "I think God has a special place for birds . . . when they die."

"Yeah," I said, knowing she had explained it as well as anyone could.

But there was this other thing that troubled me: Not only had I killed the bird, but I had also lost a good friend, even if she was a girl. I was too ashamed to ask her about that.

I wonder what she would have said.

MIRACLE DRUGS

Even when you listen attentively to what those who have spent a lifetime raising sheep have to say and read every book on the subject you can get your hands on, you can still make mistakes.

The first year I planned on having only a few lambs. I figured that if I lost any through ignorance it would not be many; I would learn as I went along. The next year I allowed myself to have quite a bunch. I was gaining in confidence and became rather proud of myself; my losses were few. I considered myself lucky.

But one Sunday morning I went down to the barn and noticed one lamb acting poorly. Its head hung low; its ears drooped. It refused to accompany the other sheep when I let them out to pasture. I left it, hoping it would get better. They sometimes do. I found myself rationalizing: If it had been in the wild, with no one to attend it, it would have to make it on its own. When I got back from church, I went immediately to the barn. The lamb still had not joined the others. It was lying on its side, looking even more poorly than before.

When I am alone I talk to myself, especially where there is a crisis and a problem to solve. I used to wonder about my doing this, glad no one was near who could hear me and perhaps think me some kind of a nut, but I later learned it is considered therapeutic to talk to yourself, just so long as you do not hear voices talking back. It's like praying, I was told.

None of the books covered what seemed to be happening here, so I called the Wilsons. No answer. By the time I returned to the barn the lamb had died. Later, when I got Betty on the phone and described all the symptoms to her, she said its death was probably caused by overeating. She called it enterotoxemia.

"But I gave it all its shots," I protested. "I gave all of them shots at the same time."

I probably sounded defensive so she did not answer right away. "Sometimes we miss," she said. "They all look alike."

But how could I have missed? I asked myself. It was quite possible, of course, but I could not admit that I had, especially to myself.

I thanked her, but when I hung up I could not help thinking about the suffering I had caused the lamb because of a possible mistake on my part. I made a vow to be more careful in the future.

Perhaps it was my way of relieving the guilt I felt that set me to thinking about what sheepherders did before there were shots for enterotoxemia and tetanus and boluses for internal parasites. It raised a whole lot of questions in my mind about how medications are used today for just about everything. Sometimes they are overused, and sometimes they are used when they should not be. Despite widespread abuse of drugs, there are any number of medications to choose from that will keep domesticated animals alive that would otherwise die. But I could not help wondering that, if they were allowed to die the way nature intended, would it not eliminate the very tendencies that cause their deaths from an increasingly weakened gene pool, since the ones that managed to survive would pass on resistances that would strengthen the breed? I suppose the same reasoning could be applied to the overuse of miracle drugs that keep people alive far beyond what nature (in its wisdom?) intends.

As I was thinking along these lines, I had to admit that mankind has benefited from the use of modern drugs, and had it been available at the time, and had my father been given insulin, he might have lived years beyond what he did and contributed much to the world. I might even have been a much different person had he lived and had I grown up under his influence. I would have been brought up in Texas or Hollywood instead of Boston, for example. But then again, I might never have known my grandmother. And I might never have heard stories about Uncle Walter and how he and I probably shared the same genetic defect.

♦

Grandma's Elderberry Wine

Grandma had seven children, three boys and four girls. Walter was her second son, born next in line after my mother. Apparently, like me, he had been full of the dickens while he was growing up, and from the way Grandma sounded, he must have been her favorite. Having to deal with him gave her about all the training she needed for handling another wild one like me when I came to live with her after spending the winter with Bert and Bill.

By then, Walter was a married man with a family of his own. I remember him as a pleasant-enough man, but he showed no hint of the fun-loving mischief maker he must have been as a boy. I think Grandma relived her delight in raising Walter through me. Her face always lit up when she told me about him and some of the wild things he did. It was as though she were reassuring me that despite my reputation as a hell raiser I would turn out all right too, if only I survived.

All of my grandma's children took music lessons, whether they had any talent or not. Mostly not. They took piano or violin—all except for my mother who, for some unexplained reason, played the mandolin.

When Walter was about the age I was when I moved back to Grandma's house—this was long before I came on the scene, of course—like all the rest, he started taking violin lessons. Apparently, he was becoming increasingly discouraged and, as a consequence, was not practicing as much as he should if he was ever to become another Fritz Kreisler. Grandma was always supportive of those who needed it and had a knack for encouraging them to extend themselves. One time, when Uncle Henningson came for Sunday dinner, she asked Walter to play.

Uncle Henningson was Grandma's uncle, an old salt who had spent so much time at sea he never settled down on any shore long enough to get married and have a family of his own. His only family was Grandma's, and he used to visit her whenever he came back from wherever he had been. I met the old boy several times before he died after we arrived from Texas in the summer of 1925. He was in his late nineties at the time. Folks lived a long time on my mother's side of the family. This was years before miracle drugs, when only the hardiest survived, passing on the strong genes.

While the rest of the kids dutifully sat around the dining room table following dessert, thankful they had not been asked to perform, Walter and Aunt Emma (the oldest, who was to accompany him on the piano) went into the living room where the piano was. Presently, the lush tones of the violin, with piano accompaniment, were heard through the open sliding doors that separated the dining room from the living room.

No one dared let on to Uncle Henningson that Walter had put a record on the gramophone of Fritz Kreisler playing his own composition, "Ziguener." Uncle Henningson, perhaps a little mellow from the elderberry wine Grandma served him with dessert, was completely taken in.

He said, with respectful awe in his voice: "By Yeesus, dot boy shuah c'n play!"

All the children had to excuse themselves from the table so Uncle Henningson could not see them struggling to keep from laughing.

Grandma had a special recipe for making elderberry wine. She made it more potent by adding raisins to it while the wine was fermenting. Just before bottling, the raisins had to be strained out. One time, Walter was helping her bottle the wine. She asked him to bury the raisins while she finished putting the stoppers in the bottles. Because the children were forbidden to drink the wine, Walter sampled a few of the raisins. He ate far too many. He got so sick he could not bury what were left over. He fed them to the chickens instead and hid for several hours to recover from involuntarily purging himself of everything he had eaten since breakfast.

Grandma discovered what he had done only when she saw the chickens staggering around, taking quick recovery steps to one side, then the other, to keep from falling, finally lolling over headfirst to lie on their sides to rest a moment before struggling valiantly to regain their feet so they could go back for more of the same.

When she told me this story she laughed until tears

came. "Oh, that Walter!" she said, wiping her eyes with her apron.

♦

Young Bucks Butting Heads

From our loft you can look out and see the sheep in the upper pasture. While the older sheep are contentedly nibbling away at the grass, the little ones are off by themselves having too much fun to bother with things like eating.

Two of the larger bucks gently butt heads. Each backs off a few feet, lowers its head, and comes charging at the other, only to ease up at the very moment when their heads touch. They are sparring, only playing at combat, because weeks before the same sort of play established, once and for all, which was to dominate the other. Had Achilles and Studley grown up together, their combat might not have ended as it did. Presently, the two young bucks join the other lambs who are busy prancing around each other like wood sprites on tiptoe.

Thinking about the lambs, Uncle Walter, and my own behavior as a child until I outgrew what was troubling me, makes me wonder about the chemistry of my youth, the process of maturing, medications, and the way science seems to be taking away the body's ability to heal itself.

I was a live-wire, wound-up, into-everything kind of kid, not unlike Uncle Walter was when he was growing up. The scientific explanation for what was wrong with me and probably him was that we were blessed with some kind of chemical imbalance. I say blessed instead of flawed because, for all its drawbacks, and there were many, whatever it was, it made us feel alive. There was nothing dull about what happened in the world when we were around.

Today, the kind of kid I was can be brought under control with medication. They give amphetamines—"speed"—to get the hyperactive kid to slow down to what society considers normal behavior. It is called a paradoxical reaction: another proof—if further proof is needed—that something was out of whack with me chemically when compared to other kids who were well behaved. There are those who would consider amphetamines the treatment of choice for the hyperactive child. I am sure the harrassed mother, teacher, or whoever is in charge of keeping such a child under control, would consider medical treatment a blessing, for it does, indeed, lessen his more rambunctious behavior. It helps the child with a short attention span to simmer down long enough to learn how to read. It also keeps him out of a lot of trouble.

But not having had such treatment when I was a kid makes me realize how lucky I was to have a mother and grandmother who were patient with me until I got over what kept me producing more than my share of the juices of youth.

A MATTER OF BREEDING

Studley is in his separate pasture looking at the ewes through the fence, the only thing that keeps him from doing the one thing he has on his mind. He stands tall, all three hundred or more pounds of him, looking like a sultan making his nightly selection. He is an impressive creature, his bearing self-assured, ready. One could say that in the animal kingdom he has noble blood, or whatever it is that gives him the appearance of elegant superiority.

He is the way he is because his parents and theirs on down the line for generations have been carefully chosen for one thing or another by breeders who were seeking to develop certain characteristics to make him look that way. Rams like Studley win all the prizes at the fair. But handsomeness, size, and conformation of body may have been achieved at the price of his breed's ability to survive without modern medications to sustain it were it suddenly thrust on its own in the wild.

Take Maxine: She is a purebred Border collie. She comes from a long line of working dogs that goes back hundreds of generations to Scotland, where the breed originated. She is a working dog, not bred for show, except that her breed is the kind most often seen putting on a show at country fairs, herding a flock of sheep into a corral.

She weighs about thirty pounds. There is nothing regal about her that judges usually look for in a show dog. But in those thirty pounds are packed an inexhaustible amount of energy that is dedicated to doing what her breed was trained to do. Work.

Were genetic engineers given the same freedom and control as dog and sheep breeders, and able to choose which human male is to mate with which human female, it is likely that over several generations this kind of selective breeding would result in offspring who would have the peculiar kinds of characteristics these scientists specifically planned to produce. All sorts of remarkable things could be accomplished: the elimination of diabetes, sickle cell anemia, even cancer, perhaps. And conceivably they could engineer twelve-foot basketball players and three-hundred-pound wide receivers who could run the hundred in nine flat. And think of the racial purity that could be achieved: all of us purebreds like Studley and Maxine.

Of course, no such program would be tolerated in a free society like ours, no matter how well intentioned those who initiated it were. But when you think about it, selective breeding is a common enough practice in real life. It is tolerated because science and the government are not telling us who to mate with. Yet, when we choose a mate we are under all sorts of pressure from outside ourselves to marry the one who is most acceptable to our families, our church, and our peers. It is less so now than several generations ago, but social, religious, and racial differences between two people, no matter how much they love each other, still influence them enough to make one or the other of them do the "right" thing.

Back when I was a kid growing up in the suburbs of Boston, there were sections that were populated exclusively by people of one nationality, race, or religion. There was Southy (South Boston), which was predominantly Irish

Catholic. (It still is, I understand.) There was the North End, where the Italians lived. There was Roslindale, where the Jews lived, and of course there was Chinatown.

As I think back to when I went to school at the Jefferson School at the bottom of the hill about a mile from my grandparents' home, I remember the mix of races, colors, religions, nationalities, languages, accents, and prejudices that made up just about all the eastern seaboard cities in the years just prior to the Great Depression of the thirties. The mix was mostly at school, rarely in the neighborhoods.

♦

Bigotry Is Taught

On one side of Parker Hill was Roxbury. On the other was Jamaica Plain. On the Roxbury side was Center Street, where the Catholic church was. It was mostly populated by Irish. Today, I understand that Roxbury is predominantly a black ghetto. (We called them Negroes then because we thought it would offend them to call them black. Times change.)

We did not consider that the Irish, the Italians, the Jews, and the blacks were forced into these separate neighborhoods because they were different; we thought they came together through their own choice, to ensure that their differences were, indeed, to remain as they were, uncontaminated by outside cultures and races. Catholics, Jews, and Protestants were forbidden to intermarry, and for a white to marry a black, even if the black was a Roman Catholic and his name was Sullivan, was unthinkable. In some states it was against the law to marry someone of another race. In other words, selective breeding was the norm.

On the Jefferson School side of the hill the neighborhood was a little less run down than on the Roxbury side. Living on top of Parker Hill we lived between the two worlds, but I was never conscious that there was more poverty on one side than the other. I am sure there was, but I was not looking for it and therefore did not see it. Perhaps anyone who might have been poor was too proud to show that he and his family was in any way disadvantaged economically. All us kids were in this youth thing together, trying too hard to be liked and accepted for ourselves alone to pay much attention to class distinction. But at an unconscious level the seeds of bigotry were being planted. I remember I was allowed, but not encouraged, to play with the kids on the Roxbury side. No reason was ever given. It was just implied. This was not a religious or racial thing so much as it was economic: It was feared I might pick up the opposite of the work ethic and slip into poverty like them.

I also remember that back in Texas if you were white and Protestant you were one of the elite. Next came white Roman Catholics, then Jews. After that came the Mexicans. Last of all came the blacks. But I was not concerned about what prejudice meant. I was trying to understand why a word that was pronounced *pred-u-diss* was spelled with a *j* and its last syllable was pronounced *diss*, as in *kiss*, and not *dice*, as in *ice*.

In other words, as far as school was concerned I was still a drudge. The other kids may not have been white and Protestant, as I was privileged to be, but they all could read and write, whereas I could not, even though I supposedly came from a superior race and creed. If anyone felt inferior it was I. Anyone who could not read was going to be dumb, and anyone who was dumb was going to be poor. Being poor was worse than being black.

♦

We Thought We Were Great

I had been kept back a couple of grades for being so dumb, and then suddenly they decided I needed to be placed in the grade where a kid my age belonged. I stood taller than any of my classmates, even the girls, who were at the age when they are taller than the boys of the same age. Skipping a couple of grades was great for my self-regard—for a while—until I fell even more behind the kids in my class academically.

The Palmer Method of teaching handwriting was then in vogue. We practiced, it seemed, endlessly. I more than the others. I labored over making my efforts precise, like everyone else's. But everyone else, especially the girls, always made their ovals and ups and downs so neatly that I was embarrassed to pass in my practice sheets with lopsided ovals, smudges, and inkblots all over them. I can honestly say that the Palmer Method did not do a thing for me except make me feel hopelessly inadequate. I probably would have done better using my left hand, as nature intended, but that was another thing wrong with me: I was a natural southpaw and they made me become right-handed.

But when it came to sports—playing ball or jumping and running around—I excelled, especially at recess. I think I was being encouraged to do more than my share of strenuous exercise in order for me to expend all my excess energy on the playground so I would be less active on my return to the classroom. It did not help much.

Another thing I did better than anyone else my age was

grow. Whenever there was a pageant commemorating some event in history, such as the Pilgrims landing at Plymouth Rock, or the First Thanksgiving, or Washington at Valley Forge, I was always cast as the lead, not for my talent but for my height. I could also be heard. When I realized that all the other kids were mumbling their lines and could not be heard beyond the first two rows, I learned to *project* (as Miss Peabody called it) by shouting.

I learned something else: Without knowing what it was called, I also learned how to dominate a scene. By thinking big I added "stature" to the character I was playing; I "projected authority"; I had "presence." If you gave me an audience I became bigger than life. When you are handicapped you tend to overcompensate in other areas.

But there was this one little kid who gave me my only real competition. He and I were the only ones who spoke loudly enough to be heard, and because the lines were written by Miss Peabody, who also directed, he and I were given all the important lines—otherwise, her immortal lines would never have been heard.

Jimmy was Italian, a wop, a dago, but we never called him either, any more than we would have called a black a nigger. He lived in an Italian area over near Plant's factory, which used to make shoes then, and later women's silk stockings. His father owned the brewery across the street from Jefferson School. It was no longer being used as a brewery because it was during Prohibition and it was now being used as a warehouse, or so it was said. It was also rumored that that was where his old man stored the booze that was shipped down from Canada in the dark of night.

Jimmy was not only sensitive about his lack of height but his dark coloring. Someone once made the mistake of calling him Blacky, which started a fight, and what Jimmy lacked in size he made up for in speed and determination.

We became the best of friends, but that did not prevent us from being rivals on stage. In October, when it was time to do our first pageant, because of his coloring Jimmy was cast as one of the Indians who welcomed Christopher Columbus when he first landed in America. All the other Indians were chosen for their coloring too. They were blacks. There were no other roles they could be cast as; Miss Peabody believed in slighting no one regardless of race, religion, or national origin.

It was then that I realized how deeply Jimmy resented his swarthy coloring—otherwise, he would not have claimed he was a direct descendent of Columbus. His name was, after all, Columbo, which somehow got changed somewhere down the line, or so he claimed. I do not think

Miss Peabody believed him any more than we did. But she took him aside and told him that he was the only Indian among the many who could be heard. He too was important, she said, to the pageant.

The following month, when the pageant for the First Thanksgiving was cast, Jimmy was again an Indian. I think the name he was given was Massasoit who, the teacher was quick to point out to Jimmy, was the most important Indian of the time and whose great generosity saved the lives of the first colonists because he taught them to bury a fish head with every grain of corn they planted.

I was John Winthrop. Again height played a part. But Jimmy was also learning how to dominate a scene. With his headdress of feathers he looked as tall as I, except when I wore that hat that was copied from the famous picture of the First Thanksgiving. It was made out of black cardboard. At dress rehearsal, as we all sat down at the table for the Thanksgiving dinner, Jimmy said to Miss Peabody, "My ma says guys ain't supposed to wear hats when yous're eatin'. Indians wore feathers all the time."

"How observant of you, James," she said, always eager to bring out the best in our poor, unfortunate, underprivileged children. (She lived out of the neighborhood, over in Chestnut Hill.) "You are quite correct," she conceded, but she hesitated because she wanted to present the tableau that was true to the famous picture. She compromised and said, "Boys, take off your hats. Only the Indians will wear their headdresses."

Jimmy gave me a look of triumph that even Miss Peabody's adding, "But James, please don't use the word ain't" couldn't erase.

But then she said, "To maintain authenticity, however, we must have John Winthrop keep his hat on. And in order to observe the rules of etiquette, he will stand up all during the scene."

Jimmy never forgave me.

I do not remember the exact dialogue Miss Peabody wrote for me as John Winthrop and Jimmy as Massasoit to speak. Perhaps it is just as well, what with Jimmy's tough street talk, spoken as though he were calling someone on the other side of town, and I, with my Texas accent, trying to outshout him, it can only be imagined what it sounded like. We thought we were great.

LOVE COMPLICATES LIFE

On weekends and during the Christmas season when school is out, sightseers from the surrounding cities often drive by while Maxie and I are out tending the sheep. They stop their cars and the occupants *ooh* and *ahh* with delight to see the lambs prancing around like a bunch of kids at recess.

Lambs really do gambol, especially when they are going downhill. They jump straight up, and when they come down on the toes of their front feet their hind legs kick off to the side, whereupon they leap up in the opposite direction. Once in a while a yearling mother, with her twins flopping along behind her like black, loose-jointed spiders, will spring up with the same exuberance of youth, only to curb her moment of impetuousness and return to behavior more befitting a young matron.

Invariably, I am asked by these curious onlookers if I raise my sheep for their wool. I usually answer, "Partly," leaving it to their imaginations what I also raise sheep for.

"You don't slaughter them, do you?" they usually exclaim in alarm when they realize what I have implied.

Since the price I get for raw wool just about equals what it costs to get the sheep sheared, I have to admit that about the only practical reason I have for raising sheep is to sell them for human consumption. "Man does not live by bread alone," I almost say. I know it would be an appropriate remark to make in this case, but that is not exactly the way Jesus meant it, so I don't. Therefore, they drive off with a look of horror on their faces as though I am some kind of murderer.

Afterwards, because I am probably defensive about it, I can usually think of any number of scathing retorts I would like to have made that do not come from the Bible. But I resist and let them go on thinking lamb chops are stamped out by machines in the back rooms of supermarkets. I let them go on denying reality because I often deny it myself; which, I suppose, is also one of nature's ways of helping us endure those things which we wish were otherwise.

For instance, nearly every year there is at least one little lamb that becomes quite friendly. At first it is tentative about it. It will sniff my pants leg and then back off, becoming bolder when it sees I mean it no harm. Sometimes, if it is a wether (a castrated ram), he will butt me in an affectionate way, usually only a gentle nudge of its head, inviting me to touch it back.

I no longer encourage lambs to get that close to me. After that first year, when the "hit man" came, I had to face the reality of having a close friend "put down." I looked off into the distance to avoid watching, but I could not keep from hearing the rifle shot go off. It is bad enough to witness the death of any creature in the springtime of life, but it is worse when it is one that has come to trust you.

Louise also gave up naming them. She names only the rams now—Stud, for example—and the ewe lambs we keep for breeding purposes.

Fudge is the oldest and one of the best bred ewes we have. She always produces twins. (She was the one that had the lamb that was brain damaged and walked funny.) Last year she gave birth to a ram and a ewe. It was a normal birth.

I made her little ram into a wether, which is what we do with rams we sell when they get to market size. But because Fudge is getting older, I decided to keep her little ewe to replace her when her producing years are over in another year or so. Louise named this little ewe Divinity, which she felt was an appropriate name for a ewe whose mother's name was Fudge. (I just tag their ears and send their numbers along with their lineage to the American Suffolk Sheep Society in order to register them as purebred Suffolks.)

Now if I had known I was going to lose Achilles in his battle with Stud, I would also have saved Fudge's little ram the indignity of castration and kept him as a replacement for his father. But unfortunately, having already done this—some things are irreversible—I had to sell him along with the rest of the market lambs.

Last night, Divinity, now ten months old, jumped the fence and got in with Stud. This morning Stud looks rather pleased with himself. Rams have a way of curling their upper lips that can be described as a cross between the lascivious sneer of a villain in one of those old-fashioned melodramas and the grin of a teenager who has just scored for the first time. Divinity is now out there baaing away as though she wants to get back in with the older but wiser girls and discuss in whatever manner they have of communicating just what the hell she has got herself into. But I notice her urge to get back in with the girls is not as great as last night's when she jumped the fence to get in with Stud. All speculation about human behavior aside, it makes one wonder which sex in the animal kingdom is the more aggressive when it comes to propagation.

Nature has a way of causing those libidinal urges to happen earlier than the sheep breeder wants them to. Therefore, I had a purpose in keeping Divinity away from Stud until late spring when I usually turn him in with the ewes in his flock. Now that she has been impregnated, Divinity will be giving birth in the early summer when it is not the right season in this part of the country to have newly born lambs because the grass will have turned brown by then. But then, love has a way of complicating life, and the mystery of it never ceases to astound me. There is an enchantment about it that makes us want to understand it. But the wonder of love is that we never do, so we keep trying.

♦

What Is Love?

When I first got Maxie all she wanted to do was herd sheep. I had to restrain her, otherwise she would not allow them time to graze. This year she does. She is learning. So am I.

Occasionally, however, she does the opposite of what she has been trained to do. Is it because she is bored or just plain ornery, similar to a child's streak of recalcitrance that is brought on by some hidden motive that is difficult to fathom? Both, perhaps. Sometimes, when I send her after a sheep that has strayed from the flock, she will go after it as she has been trained to do, but when she gets to it she will get this stupid expression on her face and act as though she does not know what she is supposed to do. She reminds me of a peasant revolting against a repressive government, or a slave and his white master—not aggressively but passively resisting by acting dumb, pretending not to know what is expected of him.

I will say, "Get up," which is the command she has been trained to obey in order to move the sheep toward me. She will get up at my command, but hesitates to advance and drive it back toward the flock. She will go up to it and lick its face as though it is one of her own litter of puppies.

I never call Maxie to me in order to reprimand her; I go to her. By my manner she knows I mean business. As I approach she makes a big show of cringing, as though she expects me to strike her, which I would never do. Not Maxie. It is as though she is trying to find out if I love her enough to make her behave. I figure she is testing my authority—or my love—like a child does when it is trying to see how much it can get away with.

I will take her by the scruff of the neck with both hands and lift her front feet about six inches off the ground and say in a gruff voice, "Behave!" I do not know if she knows what *behave* means, but she understands what I mean by the sternness of my voice. For the rest of the time we are out with the sheep—and generally for the next week or so—she will do all I tell her without hesitation. Apparently, it is necessary for her security—or whatever—that I reestablish every once in a while that I am still the one in charge. Perhaps she has a wisdom that passes human understanding that recognizes that it is I, her master, who also needs reassurance as to who is boss.

I once saw a blind man with a large German shepherd holding on to the harness while the dog led him down the sidewalk. The dog stopped them at the intersection until the light changed so they could cross safely. It was the first time I had ever seen a Seeing Eye dog in action. I was most impressed. But while they waited at the bus stop, the blind man, seated on the bench while the dog lay on the sidewalk at his feet, jerked the harness sharply to reprimand the dog. I could not tell what the dog had done wrong—it looked to be acting superbly to me—but, apparently, it was misbehaving in some way that only its master and it was aware of. I thought: How insensitive the blind man is being to such a proven friend, whose loyal service to him was incalculable.

But since Maxie sometimes feels she needs to test me, I now realize that discipline may be a form of love that needs to be proven from time to time, otherwise it might be taken for granted. Ask anyone which teacher he admired most, and he will invariably say it was the one who demanded the most from him, although he would not be likely to admit it at the time.

I do not suppose it makes much sense to wonder if Maxie herds sheep because she loves me or if she does it because she loves to herd sheep. I know she loves me, but she also loves to herd sheep. It is all so simple for her: Like God, Maxie *is* love. Human love can be so much more complicated.

By *love* I do not mean the feeling we get when we fall in love. That kind of love is rather straightforward and to the point, having more to do with lust. Science tells us there is a chemical we produce which makes us feel horny, and that some people produce more phenethylamine than others. Infatuation has no more to do with LOVE (uppercase) than it does when Maxie or Divinity wants to make love (lowercase) with any dog or ram that happens to be around at the time. (The location of cases here is an interesting coincidence.) What we often call love is made complicated because we sometimes mix lowercase love with uppercase LOVE. I will be the first, however, to affirm that one can lead to the other, which is probably the way it is meant to be for a lot of reasons.

♦

Young Love

When I take the sheep out to graze it attracts attention, a sure way of getting to know the neighbors. Some rather well. This year there is one neighbor in particular. I know she loves me for she brings me wild flowers she picks on her way to greet me. She is so loving I cannot help but return her love. Even though this affair has gone on for a couple of months it has to end. It is not that I am an old married man. It is her age. She is only three.

The young are so open about the love they give; they scatter it like pollen. But I know from past experience that in time she will outgrow the love she has for me. Several years ago I had another girlfriend. She lives on our mountain and was about the same age then as my current girlfriend is now. She was much more aggressive than this one: Rather than bring me flowers, she came right out and told me she loved me.

But, alas, she does not even come out to greet me anymore. All she does now is wave to me from the window when we pass by her house. She is more interested in watching TV and playing second base for one of the Little League teams in the village than she is in me.

This morning, after her mother called my new girlfriend indoors when it began to rain and we moved beyond her house, it left me alone with Maxie, the sheep, and my thoughts. As I leaned against a tree to protect myself from the light rain, again my thoughts turned to love. Young love.

When I was in the fifth grade at Jefferson School we would go over to the nearby quarry and watch the workmen drill holes in the stone, into which dynamite charges were placed. The all-clear whistle wailed. It sounded more shrill and urgent than the lonely call of a train whistle. And while we watched from a safe distance on the opposite rim of the quarry, the explosion would go *whumphf!* and a cascade of crumbling rocks would slide down onto the quarry floor. These huge boulders had to be reduced to smaller stones. This was done by dropping a metal ball, about two feet in diameter, hoisted by a crane, on the rocks. The crane was powered by a steam engine, operated by a man we could see inside his glassed-in compartment, pulling a multitude of levers with both hands with a dexterity we thought remarkable.

Once, when Jimmy Columbo and I were at our usual place where we could watch the activity out of harm's way, the operator motioned us over. Such admiration from two worshippers had to be acknowledged. He asked us questions about school, what our ages were, and our names. When Jimmy told him his, the man said he must be Italian. Remarkable, we thought, because Jimmy did not have an Italian accent. But when I told him mine and he said I was of German descent, we thought this even more remarkable because I had a southern accent. We were both mighty impressed; we thought he was a very smart man.

Another time, when I was alone and there was a lull in the work, the man waved me over. I clambered down, went over and stood looking up at him in his monstrous machine. And wonder of wonders, he invited me inside. I climbed the metal ladder and sat next to him while he showed me how each lever and foot pedal made the crane go up and down and to the left and right. He was a large man with a bull neck, but his face and voice were gentle. His size reminded me of what little I remembered of my father. I could tell he was a nice man, that he liked kids.

"I'll bet you'd like to run one of these when you grow up," he said.

"Wow!" I said. "Would I!"

"How about now?"

"Now?"

"Just pull this lever. I'll tell you when to push it back."

As I did, I got this feeling of great power; I could actually cause this huge erector set to reach for the sky.

"Now, push it forward," he said. "That's enough." It stopped. He worked the foot pedals. "Now, push it forward again. That's enough."

He worked another lever. The hook descended until it reached the ground. One of the men came over and attached the hook onto the metal ball. After the man moved away, my newfound friend worked a lever to make the ball rise slowly into the air. He made several minor adjustments, sounded the all-clear signal, and then said in a soft voice, "When I tell you, pull this lever."

How could he be so calm, I asked myself, when I was so excited. If only Jimmy could see me now!

I pulled it. The hook released it and the ball came crashing down to shatter the rocks below in a shower of dust and shards of splintered stone.

He smiled. "That's not hard, is it?"

He may not have known it, but this man did a lot for me. He made me realize that even though I would never be any good at reading and writing, I could be a crane operator, or at least the one who hooked the ball onto the cable.

I know I must have loved this man. I suppose I still do—at least, I love the memory of him. I worshipped him the way boys do a big-league ball player, the way my present girlfriend who brings me flowers loves me.

When I told Jimmy about operating the machine he would not believe me. His disbelief was confirmed when the man failed to ask either of us over, even to talk. I guess he was told by management not to risk having kids that close to danger anymore. He merely waved to us after that. We always waved back, hoping he would ask us over to talk to him.

After a while I quit going to watch him perform his magic, for I, too, found other interests, the way my former girlfriend who had told me she loved me has found hers. I suppose young love can sometimes seem fickle, but after all these years I realize I still feel affection for someone I once loved, even if I no longer remember his name.

◆

"You Look So Beautiful Tonight"

The second year after I moved back into my grandparents' home, Aunt Helen (the youngest of my mother's sisters) and her husband, Tom, and their only child, Donald, came to live with Grandma too. There was enough room despite her taking in boarders. She was great when it came to taking people in who needed it. And Aunt Helen and Uncle Tom really were in need.

Uncle Tom had a drinking problem. He was very handsome, easygoing, and much more fun-loving than interested in working. He had not gone to college. He did not need to for he was a salesman, and apparently a good one when he was sober. He had a gift of letting people know he liked them, which, of course, made them like him and want to be around him. He loved to laugh and make other people laugh. But most of all he loved to drink, which, I suppose, was part of his charm, but also his downfall.

He was also thoughtful: He took me to my first big-league baseball game. We lived about three miles from Fenway Park. It was the Red Sox playing the mighty New York Yankees. The Red Sox won that day even though Babe Ruth was in the lineup for the Yankees. He went 0 for 4. I have followed the Red Sox ever since, being a great one for picking almost winners. No other team over the past fifty years have I followed with greater hope, only to have those expectations shattered on the last day of the season (usually to the Yankees), the last day of the playoffs, or the last batter up in the last inning of the seventh game of the World Series.

One time, when Uncle Tom came home and his eyes were particularly bright, his voice cheerful, his manner more loving and mellow than usual, Donald—then only about five—asked me in a whisper, "Is my father drunk?" There was fright in his voice along with concern. I did not know what to answer. I said, "No, he's just happy to be home." I wanted to protect Donald, but I also wanted to protect Uncle Tom. (Why are we always so protective of drunks, and why do we always love them, even though they always let us down and break our hearts? I have always associated the Red Sox with Uncle Tom.)

Uncle Tom was also religious on occasion, although I do not remember his going to church on a regular basis. He was a Catholic, being Irish. All Grandma's girls married Irish Catholics except my mother. I suppose Uncle Tom felt that anyone who was Protestant was suspect and needed all the help he could get because one time he asked if I had ever been baptized. (I had been, of course, as an infant.) I said I did not remember, which was a mistake, for he was scandalized to hear me confess that it was possible that I had never been and I was going straight to hell if I didn't.

He immediately took me to the kitchen sink and with water from the tap he proceeded to baptize me (in extremis) in the name of the Father, and of the Son, and of the Holy Ghost. He was very serious about it. He was also drunk. He had probably gotten into Grandma's elderberry wine. Again.

That is how I got baptized twice. Uncle Tom's probably was not as binding as the first, but it made more of an impression on me than the one I could not remember. His was also done in LOVE.

But he gave Aunt Helen a rough time of it all her life. He was always getting fired from one job after another. But as I said, he had this other side, which was never brought home to me quite so strongly as an event I recall that took place years later.

By then he had joined AA, which he attended regularly —at times, he later confessed, even when he was drunk. It was the first chapter started in the Boston area. AA helped him put together longer periods of sobriety so that he stuck with one company long enough to earn enough to buy a home in Jamaica Plain.

It was during the Second World War. Both Donald and I were in the armed forces, soon to be on our way overseas. Mother had moved to a tiny apartment on Beacon Street by then, and my sister was married to a marine officer and was living with him in Quantico. I was on leave, and Helen and Tom invited mother and me to have Sunday dinner at their house.

I chanced upon a scene I will never forget. While I was on my way to the bathroom, passing the opened door to their bedroom, I overheard Tom say to Helen, "You look so beautiful tonight." They were unaware of my passing by, and I would have missed it if I had come by a moment before or after.

I caught a glimpse of Aunt Helen's face. Her expression was one of utmost joy and tenderness toward this truly flawed man she had chosen to stick with despite a lifetime of his continued drunkenness and probable unfaithfulness. I am sure an attractive man such as he, who could get people to love him so easily and who was, of course, a very weak man, would surely have had many affairs. It was hinted at that he had. His being an alcoholic was no excuse for that, of course, but then, perhaps he had to prove something to himself in that way because he considered himself a failure in others. Yet, how many men are so lucky as he to have had someone love him as Helen did? And did he appreciate her? I like to think she thought he did. That he needed her there is no doubt, but perhaps she needed him to misbehave just to prove to him and to herself how much she loved him, just as Maxie must sometimes test my love for her.

"PRAYER DOESN'T CHANGE GOD, JUST MAN"

Several experiences during my formative years gave me a love for the land and for growing things. They gave me an appreciation of nature and the wonder of it. One experience in particular made me aware of how the farmer comes to rely on a Power outside himself to help him explain away and endure the precariousness of natural events that make his life anything but easy.

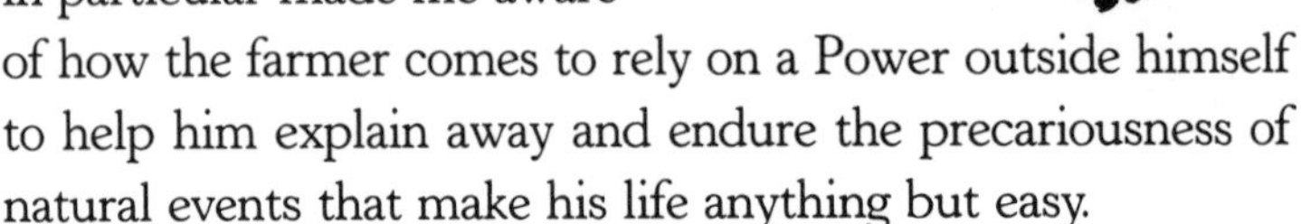

One of my mother's childhood friends was married to a man who's father owned and worked one of the few remaining farms located very near to Boston. It was outside the town of Dedham; today there is probably a shopping center where it once was.

My mother's chum Elsie had five children. Her oldest boy, George, and I became the best of friends. It was suggested that we city boys spend a summer on his grandfather's farm on the outskirts of Dedham. Old man Eagles could use our help, we were told.

When it became apparent I was not going to be a scholar (and a career as a farmer was an alternative for a dumb kid like me), it seemed to them a way of introducing me to farm life to see how I liked it. (They did not know I wanted to be a crane operator along about then. And then, of course, I also knew I could also be a fireman or a policeman if the crane operator job did not work out.)

We worked hard that summer earning our keep. There were rows of weeds to be hoed under the hot sun. We got blisters, but they quickly turned to callouses. We fed the stock and the chickens and swilled the hogs. We even milked the cows. It was before milking machines came into general use. Hay balers were not much in evidence either. Hay had to be pitched by hand with long-handled pitchforks up onto a wagon drawn by a team of horses, which George and I took turns driving to the barn, where the hay was lifted up to the loft by means of a rope pulled through a pulley that was suspended from the roof beam. Now there is nothing like haying to work up a sweat and give you a dry mouth, but there is nothing on God's green earth more refreshing than a drink from a metal dipper of cold, clear water you have just pumped by hand from a well.

But it was not all work. We had time to roam the hills and meadows. We snuck through the forests pretending to be any number of imagined characters. We were Indian scouts, trappers, or hunters stalking real and imagined game. We were city boys discovering the magic of nature, exploring the wonder of our imaginations. We breathed the cool, moist odors of the forest floor and the strangely sweet-smelling hot dry dust kicked up as we walked barefooted over parched dirt roads.

Then there was the joy of riding the workhorses bareback to the pond for them to drink and for us to swim at the end of the day. And after dinner (country folks called it supper; dinner was at noon) we would sit in the cool of the evening on the porch discussing any number of subjects, mostly the crops and the livestock and our immediate problem: our need for rain.

It had been a particularly dry summer, the worst in years, we were told. The old folks would make comments like, "If it don't rain soon the crops'll dry up," and "We'll have a poor harvest this fall, sure 'nuff." Answered by, "Yea-ah," in that uniquely New England way of expressing agreement.

Thus, rain became a matter of survival, not just an annoying inconvenience which on previous summers could spoil a perfectly good sunshiny day at the beach, a picnic, or a ball game.

I do not remember our ever going to church the whole summer. Not that it mattered: Protestants always take the summer off from church. Church was beginning to bore me anyway, and I was not about to bring it up for fear I would have reminded them and they would make George and me go. But grace was said at every meal.

As the drought grew more critical, I noticed the old man got an edge to his voice as he thanked God for the food we were about to receive. It was not an offhand sort of grace; the old man sounded as though he really meant it. His prayers became more urgent with each succeeding meal. And after a while I found myself silently throwing in a few fervent wishes (prayers) of my own. I went so far as to bargain with God that I would be a better behaved boy and stay out of mischief in exchange for one good thunderstorm. I was willing to settle for a small shower, even a drizzle. Like a lot of people I was beginning to think that my behavior, and how hard I prayed, had a bearing on whether I got what I wanted from God.

Our prayers for rain were eventually answered, of course. It seems that if you wait long enough it always does, which tends to make you think it is your prayers that have caused it.

What makes me think along these lines is that right now I hear the sheep baaing away, reminding me it is time I fed them. There is no rain here during the summer and I usually feed them alfalfa in the morning and afternoon until the rain comes, when they have green grass to graze on again. And as I sit here writing about my summer on the Eagles' farm and hearing the sheep in the background, I find myself concocting some sort of Kafkaesque story about my sheep turning to me, their only source of survival, praying I will not forget them in their hour of need; and that the harder they beg the more likely I will give in and do what they want. The longer I take to put these thoughts down, the louder they beg. I know that as soon as I feed them they will bleat no more until they need me again, for their "prayers" will have again been answered for the time being. But what a comfort it must be for them to know I can always be relied on, because their prayers, if prayers they be, have always been answered in the past. Can it be that they feel it is their prayers alone that prompts me to do what they want?

One dry spell, answered just in time by prayed-for rain, does not—for reasons I just hinted at—a convert make. That summer, so very long ago, when I was just beginning to ask similar questions about a lot of things, I became aware of a farmer's reliance upon God, "from whom all blessings flow," when one lives as close to the earth as he does. I discovered that he finds comfort in his belief that there is, indeed, a Power outside himself he can call upon in times of crisis. I ask myself: Where's the harm in that? Without faith mankind would probably despair and give up. I think it was Kierkegaard who said that prayer does not change God, just man.

♦

What Does *X* Mean?

When I returned to the city at the end of the summer I was told I was to go to the Hillside School, a private school just outside Marlborough, about thirty-five miles from Boston. It was a school that taught boys how to become responsible adults who could support themselves. Central in its training was that each boy was given a chore he was expected to perform every day in addition to tending to his personal hygiene and making his own bed. No boy was ever given a task he could not do, and, therefore, there was no excuse for malingering. As a result there was no malingering that I was ever aware of.

The interesting thing about doing all these chores was that each of us discovered that the more difficult the task assigned him, the greater was his pride in accomplishing it. We knew we would be given an even more responsible job after we had proven ourselves, and by working ourselves up the work ladder we became even more important in the eyes of others and ourselves. By graduating from simple tasks to the more difficult ones we acquired skills that were ordinarily done by adults in the real world. It was something we worked toward, like a promotion with more pay. Only we did not get paid. It was approval we sought. We were being taught the work ethic without our knowing that was what it was called. Perhaps even more important was that he who was poor in school could establish his worth as a person by working in those areas where he did best. And by the time we graduated from the eighth grade, those who would not go on to high school would be assured a job as a farmhand. The Great Depression had just started and considerations such as one's economic survival were uppermost in everyone's minds.

I am sure that this was what appealed to my mother's practicality, or whoever else's was involved in the decision-making process that determined that Hillside was where I belonged.

The school was, for the most part, self-supporting. It raised its own cattle, chickens, vegetables; preserved its own fruits; canned its own beets, beans, tomatoes, and corn; and picked its own apples. All these farm chores were under the supervision of Pop Sanford, the school's principal, and a couple of hired hands. We learned the basic skills of farming from them.

Not only did Hillside teach us how to earn our own living, but it gave us a basic education. We were taught the old-fashioned way: the sixth, seventh, and eighth grades were all taught in the same room and had only one teacher, Mrs. Sanford, the principal's wife. She could not have come into my life at a better time. She exposed us to all the world's best literature and made us like it. Those of us who were poor readers were not forced to read it by ourselves. She took a portion of each school day to read to us aloud: Dickens, Mark Twain, Terhune, Tarkington, and all the classics boys love. And by reading to us the likes of *Ivanhoe,*

The Deerslayer, The Legend of Sleepy Hollow, we were as enriched as those who could read them to themselves. She had us learn "by heart" the soliloquies of *Hamlet* and *Macbeth* and Portia's speech that "The quality of mercy is not strain'd; it droppeth as the gentle rain from heaven," and the poem *Hiawatha*. I can still hear its rhythms beginning with "BY the SHORES of GIT-chee-GU-mee" and recite most of it from memory, even though I now cannot always remember what I had for lunch the day before.

And the kind of arithmetic she taught dealt with the basics and was made relevant: "If a scoop of grain holds X number of pounds, how many scoops are there in a hundred-pound bag?"

She invited class participation. But we always had to raise our hands to be called on, which we were more than eager to do, especially if we knew the answer. But since she seldom called on the same one twice in a row, even if we did not know the answer, we would raise our hands to give her the impression that we knew it.

"What does *X* mean?" one of the kids asked.

"Does anyone know? Yes, Jim?"

"It means ten?" Jim said.

"It means ten if its a Roman numeral," Mrs. Sanford said. "It can also mean an unknown quantity. In this case it does. How are you going to find out how much a scoop weighs?"

she asked. All of us had an answer for that and raised our hands.

"Take a scoopful and weigh it," said the one she called on.

"Good. Now, say a scoop of grain weighs two pounds. How do you find out how many scoops in a hundred-pound bag?"

"Fifty," a couple of the kids blurted out.

"Wait until you're called upon," she warned. "How did you arrive at that number?"

"By dividing two into one hundred."

"Correct."

If one or more of the kids had an uncomprehending expression on his face, she went over it again. "Now, let us say you have thirty cows and you feed each a scoop of grain at milking time twice a day. . ." And so on.

She was also a pianist. Each morning we sang a number of old favorites from a songbook each of us had in his desk. She plunked away at the piano while we sang, "The Old Oaken Bucket," "The Spanish Cavalier," "Santa Lucia," "America the Beautiful," and all the other old favorites.

We also recited the Pledge of Allegiance, after which we read aloud a different psalm each day. That was the extent of our religious training in the classroom. But just prior to having dinner each night we all knelt beside our chairs and recited the Lord's Prayer.

Each Sunday, however, we were all taken to church in town. Most of us were of the Protestant faith and went to church with the Sanfords. A few went to the Roman Catholic church, but another boy and I were chosen to go to another church across town for reasons I will tell about shortly. There were also two boys who were Jewish. While I do not recall, they were probably taken to their services on Friday nights.

♦

"Lo! The Angel of the Lord Appears!"

Even if a deer were to come near the house to dine on Louise's roses, Maxie will not chase it until I tell her. All she does is bark. One warning yip is enough to let the deer know that the roses are for us, not for it. The rest of the time Maxie lies waiting, always waiting, listening for the sounds I make inside the house, telling of my presence.

In the morning, when she hears the toilet flush, her ears perk up. I descend the stairs, go to the kitchen, return to the dining room to have breakfast, then back upstairs to brush my teeth, and down again.

It is on my second descent—the Second Coming, so to speak—that she stands up with certainty that now, at last, her messiah is to appear. She meets me at the kitchen door, tail wagging, making little squeaking sounds of delight.

I go to the garage, and while I am changing from my slippers into rubber boots her body squirms back and forth as though she is hinged at the middle, impatient for me to get my boots on so she can race down to the barn, where I will open the gate and she can lead the sheep and me out into the open. Like all young things, she is having to learn to control her exuberance.

She has my sympathy. It was not easy for me to control myself either. I suppose no child finds it easy, but it was more difficult for me, being hyperactive. I can remember a number of occasions when I was growing up when losing control became embarrassing. But at least Maxie is unable to laugh or blush. It was Mark Twain who said, "Man is the only animal that blushes. Or needs to."

At Hillside School it was discovered I had a voice. And, of course, I love music. As sheep are to Maxie, music is to me. It was only a matter of time before Mrs. Sanford had me singing solos at performances the school gave from time to time.

My first opportunity to perform came the first year I was at Hillside. It was just before we returned to our home for

Christmas vacation. I was the Angel of the Lord who appeared before the shepherds to tell them of the birth of the Christ child and again in the tableau of the Nativity scene with the baby Jesus in a manger, surrounded by the shepherds and the Three Wise Men. Three of the oldest boys, whose voices had only recently changed, sang "We Three Kings of Orient Are." Occasionally, and without warning, their recently acquired manly voices shifted upward to a preadolescent treble, which lent the only suspense to the oft-told tale.

I wore a long white gown and a headband that supported a golden halo that encircled the back of my head. It bobbed and shimmered in the bright lights in all its flickering glory. I sang, "Lo! the Angel of the Lord appears . . ." with what I heard Mrs. Sanford say to someone was a voice that sounded as true as a bell. I was able to reach the highest notes with the purity and effortlessness of youth. I could reach an *F* above high *C* without straining. It was as easy for me as breathing. And if I wanted to attract someone's attention at a distance, instead of calling to them I could trill at the top of my voice and make it sound like a police whistle. I could do just about anything with my voice, except when the music got to me.

One time in rehearsal I got so moved by the beauty of

the music I was singing, nothing came out except a croak. Some people are easily brought to tears when affected by emotion; with me it is my throat: I choke up. I had to stop. I could not let on how I felt; a boy is not supposed to show he has feelings. That kind. It was all part of learning how to control your emotions. But around that time, when it came to controlling my emotions, along with just about everything else, I was a mess.

Mrs. Sanford must have understood. She excused me to go get a drink of water. When I came back I sang the song as it was supposed to be sung in all its virginal purity. Angels are not supposed to have emotions.

It was in formal situations, however, when I had to keep still, that I had my greatest problem. Most hyperactive children outgrow it. I was still working on it.

♦

I Get Paid for Going to Church

The Protestant church most of the kids at Hillside attended followed closely the traditions of our Pilgrim forefathers. Their services tended to be severe, without emotion, except when the preacher was preaching about sin, which was just about all I ever remember him preaching about. No ostentation was allowed. Even the architecture was austere. Some of the churches of this denomination considered decorations of any kind—even flowers—excessive, nor did they allow organs, because they were not mentioned in the Bible. (I hope that particular denomination has lightened up a bit since then; its tendency toward narrowness lost me.)

One Sunday the first year I was at Hillside, the minister was preaching about hell and damnation. What else? He was getting himself all worked up and, at the most dramatic moment, at the top of his voice, in which he condemned all who did not follow the narrow path of moral rectitude, predicting all would go straight to hell if we did not, his bridgework popped out of his mouth. Luckily, he caught it just before it hit the pulpit and was able to shove it back in soon enough to go on shouting about his favorite subject. But this struck me as being funny.

Others in the congregation thought it funny too, but none of them laughed; they had spent their lifetimes in church learning how to be stern and not show any emotion, particularly in a situation like this. The boys around me who tittered got control of themselves soon enough; they did not dare do otherwise. But me, poor me: While they were able to stifle little choking sounds inside bodies that shook all over, I had to slip down under the pew in front of me to get out of sight and hold my sides to keep from laughing out loud. As soon as I got control of myself, one of my schoolmates would stifle a snicker, which was all it took to start the whole excruciating process over again. It seemed an hour before I had exhausted myself enough to get complete control. By then the sermon was over. But not my shame.

Shortly thereafter, my belief in a redeeming instead of an angry and vindictive God began. Another boy and I escaped the fellowship of this righteous bunch of Puritans and got to go to a church where they served wine (during Prohibition, yet!) instead of grape juice at communion and where there was song instead of unremitting guilt. I am sure they acknowledged that there was such a thing as sin and guilt, but I heard less about it there than I had at the other church. Our Pilgrim and Puritan forebears escaped the Church of England and found freedom of worship in the Land of the Free; I only had to go across town to reverse the process and find another kind of freedom in a place where going to church was fun.

This denomination, following the traditions of the Church of England from which it originated, liked to have boys' choirs. Boys who can carry a tune and have musical ability are not always in great number in their churches, however. But that does not stop them from wanting to sound like Westminster Abbey. Therefore, they have a policy of recruiting boys from other denominations. One's faith and moral character are never a primary consideration, but a God-given talent is. It is not without price, however; I was paid the vast sum of a quarter every time I sang a solo. That was in addition to the quarter the other boy and I were each paid for just showing up and doing what we liked best. Moreover, the collection plate was never passed among the choir members, so I was not confronted with that dilemma, which by now I had resolved. In fact, I had the best of all possible worlds: I was being paid for going to church, which would have been mandatory anyway; and I was also paid to sing, which I would have done for nothing.

♦

I Become a Christian for the Third Time

I also got to hear a different kind of sermon. I remember one in particular. I do not remember the exact words, of course, so I will give a brief summary.

The text was from Matthew: The head of the ruler's

house is told that his daughter is dead. Jesus says to him: "Depart; for the girl is not dead but sleeping." Everyone scoffs at Him, but Jesus takes her by the hand and she arises. Everyone says it is a miracle.

The preacher said that we could call what Jesus did a miracle if we wanted, but that was not the point. It was really about forgiveness, and how it relates to miracles.

He then explained that the church in those days, and for the past thousand years or so, believed in retributive justice, which meant that the punishment must fit the crime, an "eye for an eye."

But what about sins that are committed in secret? Easy, he said: When someone got sick or misfortune befell him, it was God's way of letting everyone know that a secret sin had been committed and, thus, God was punishing him for his wrongdoing. But when he recovers from the illness or his misfortune passes, it is believed that the guilty one has been punished enough, and God has forgiven him.

Therefore, when Jesus heals people and says to them, "Your sins are forgiven, go and sin no more," the religious leaders of the day figure Jesus is making himself equal with God, for they believe that only God can forgive sins. This they considered blasphemy. The punishment for blasphemy was death.

The preacher further explained that what Jesus was saying was that everyone of us has it within his power to heal, to forgive sins. Forgiving is not God's prerogative alone. We too can heal by loving, by caring, by forgiving those who have wronged us. By healing them we ourselves are healed. This was the Good News I kept hearing so much about in church, but which I now had *heard* for the first time. Even though I had been baptized twice, once as an infant and again at the kitchen sink by my Uncle Tom, it was somewhere around then I guess you could say I really became a Christian.

There was the added benefit of having someone from church pick us up at school on Thursday evenings and take us to choir practice. Often we were taken to dinner at their homes beforehand. Even though we were fed well enough by the school, which raised its own food, it was a welcome break from institutional cooking. Home cooking and the warmth of nice, decent, and loving people, each on his best behavior, is a treat that is hard to equal when one is away from home.

Sometimes, after the Sunday service, we stayed in town and had dinner at different people's homes. This also meant we would have supper with them as well because we were to sing Evensong, which is probably one of the loveliest services in all Christendom, but is rarely performed anymore. Afterwards, we would be driven back to school, sated with good food and overflowing with good feelings about small-town people who are well intentioned and the sounds of "Abide with me: fast falls the eventide," and the Nunc Dimittis, sung to the J. Barnby setting, still lingering in our minds.

Some boys who were members of the congregation and sang in their choir with us had sisters who were about the same age as we. And being starved as we were for female companionship, just to have these delightful creatures, these visions of feminine loveliness, seated across the table from us, was enough to make us mind our manners and feel overprivileged and a little guilty for having been blessed with more pleasant voices than the other kids at school.

During services on Sunday I would look out and see these creatures from another world. They would be seated demurely in their pews, sneaking looks back at me with shy but delighted eyes that let me know we were thinking the same things, but which we knew we could do nothing about. Such things would have to wait.

KEEP YOUR OPTIONS OPEN

One of my neighbors has an observatory. It overlooks the pond and is on the highest hill atop the Tularcitos Ridge. Bob is an airline pilot, an accomplished organist, and an amateur astronomer. I suppose if he were an athlete as well he would be considered a Renaissance man. He lives somewhere near the Carmel Highlands. But as often as he can, when he is not flying, he comes out at night when the moon is not out and peers at the stars through his huge telescope and takes pictures of them. The telescope is rigged to move mechanically at whatever speed is necessary to keep pace with the earth's rotation in order to keep the distant star he is observing within his field of vision. Otherwise, he would have to keep moving the whole thing by hand once in a while. In other words, it is the latest thing as far as astronomical observation is concerned. Professional.

The observatory, I am told, is placed on one of the most ideal sites you can find in the world for this sort of thing. The weather conditions are such that when the valley below us fills with fog, and the ridge above is clear, it causes the atmosphere to stabilize and shimmer less up here than elsewhere.

After spending so many years in the Los Angeles basin, where the temperature inversion obscures the night sky so that the stars are seen through a yellow filter of smog, a night does not pass when I do not walk along our road and feel blessed that I can again experience the bright skies of my youth. Even when there is no moon the stars are bright enough for me to walk with Maxie along our road without need of any light other than that reflected from the stars.

I remember such a night when I was still at Hillside. I could not have been more than twelve. When I got up to go to the bathroom, I looked out the window and saw a huge star burning a hole in the sky. From its center were four thrusts of light forming a perfect cross. I had not seen anything like it except on Christmas cards.

I was in awe of what I beheld. Surely, I thought, this was an omen of great importance. It had to be shared. Witnessed. Verified.

I woke my classmates. They too experienced the wonder of it with exclamations of, "Wow! Super! *Jesus*, will you look at *that*!—I mean, '*Gee*, look at that, will ya!'"

One of the boys went outside for a better look, and our short-lived joy was crushed by the pressure of reality. He said something like: "Hey, you guys, it's nothin' but a lousy old star."

What we had seen from inside was the same star (or more precisely a planet, probably Venus), but the still, unpainted copper window screens, replaced the day before, created an optical illusion, and our impressionable, trusting, wanting-to-believe young eyes had tricked us into thinking we had seen a miracle.

This was years before they had plastic screens and the next day the screens were painted to keep them from rusting. Our star of wonder had been painted over with black paint, never to be seen in quite the same way again. It was, however, a kind of miracle. For me, at least. I found I could still feel childlike enchantment at a time when I was beginning to take everyday miracles for granted.

Yet, I had every reason to keep my options open because, surely, a miracle was happening to me. My lazy brain finally began to function the way it was supposed to. Word symbols on the printed page began to be transmitted to that part of my brain that comprehends what they are supposed to mean. It took me about an hour to read a page, but by the time I finished I knew its meaning. Reading was such slow going I had to make a special effort to keep from daydreaming. But my need for fantasizing diminished the more I learned to read. The written word became exciting because I did not know what was coming next unless I could read the next page to find out. I also knew that if I did not keep at it I would be saddled with a life of illiteracy, and that did not fit in with my dreams of greatness that I suppose all kids have.

Because many of us attending Hillside would not go beyond the eighth grade, Mrs. Sanford taught us to name the parts of speech, to parse sentences, and how to write them. The Palmer Method of writing was not taught, however; she did not believe in it. We just wrote as best we could because more important to her than legibility was proper sentence construction, content, and a logical progression from the topic sentence to the conclusion. "Write what you want to say," she kept writing in the margins of our compositions.

I am forever grateful to that woman, because when I finished Hillside it became apparent that I was not destined to become a young farmhand after all, but a high school student. She had prepared me for it. Well, almost.

♦

But a Scholar I'm Not

The high school nearest my grandparents' home was The Boston Latin School, the oldest (it is older than Harvard College) and one of the most prestigious public schools in the country. On the other side of the street was the High School of Commerce, which emphasized basic business skills, such as typing, shorthand, and bookkeeping. One was for the scholar—who would probably go on to Harvard University (or some such worthy institute of higher learning, which catered to the elite of the academic world)—and the other for the less scholarly, who would graduate into the business world at the lowest rung of the commercial ladder.

Entering students had to take an entrance exam to get into Boston Latin. None was required at the other. I took the exam. When it came time to examine my reading ability I was understandably anxious. I remember having to sit across the desk from this older, gray-haired woman. She was kindly looking, with a nice, grandmotherly smile—probably a retired teacher. She could see I was nervous and immediately tried to put me at ease, as she probably had all the others. She opened a book for me to read. I read the page aloud. Haltingly, of course. I am sure it took me much longer than any of the other kids, but I managed to get to the bottom of the page without missing a word. I thought she was going to end it right there because I had read so poorly, but she asked me to tell her what I remembered having read.

"Word for word?"

"No, dear, what did it say? What was it about?"

I told her it was about pigeons that tumbled in the air when they flew.

She smiled and thanked me. I knew I was probably the slowest and poorest sight reader she had ever heard in all her years of teaching, but she made me feel I had done very well. I could see she liked kids. She made me feel confident I was going to be accepted as an entering student at Boston Latin.

But then reality set in. Here we were in the midst of the deepest depression in the history of our country, and I knew I would need to get a job as soon as I could. I would have to forego college because I knew mother could not afford to send me to one. And I knew for sure I was not going to get into college on my brains. Football, maybe, or track, but not on an academic scholarship. As I began to think about it, I realized that at Boston Latin I would be required to take four years of Latin. But not only that, I would have to take at least one year of classical Greek and three years of French or German. I was having enough trouble as it was learning to read English; just think what a burden it would have been having to read three foreign languages as well. Moreover, it was rumored that only about three out of five entering students graduated. I would not have had a chance.

As luck would have it, the decision was taken out of my hands. I was not accepted. As I think back, remembering the kind of pressure I was already under trying to catch up with the other kids academically, I know I would have failed. My years of illiteracy had made me feel most inadequate. It was this, I suppose, as much as anything else, that made me seek acceptance anywhere I could. I would not have been accepted at Boston Latin. I would have felt as if I were in a world of geniuses.

"MAKE BELIEVE"

Even when you get better control of your mind, there are times when your body does what you do not want it to. Like when you blush. It always seems to get worse the more I try not to.

After I graduated from Hillside and was again living with my mother at my grandparents' house, Aunt Helen and Donald were also living at Grandma's. Uncle Tom was in Buffalo at some job where he was supposed to send for Helen and Donald "when he got settled in his job."

One afternoon, Helen and I were alone in the house. Mother

was at work, Grandma was probably out shopping, and Donald, who was about ten years younger than I, was out playing.

Aunt Helen was my mother's youngest sister, then in her late twenties. I thought she was ancient. She was very pretty, petite, fragile-looking, and soft. At the age of sixteen I towered over her. You did not think of her as the kind of girl who *made* love; she was the kind you made love *to*.

There are rites of passage in every culture. In ours, when I was growing up, one of them was when you learned to dance well enough to steer a girl (who was just as scared as you) around the dance floor without making a fool of yourself. It was Aunt Helen who taught me to dance.

She used to get the old 78s and we would play them on the Victrola, the kind you had to wind with a crank and had to change the needle after every couple of playings. They were the romantic love ballads of Rogers and Hart, the Gershwins, Irving Berlin, Cole Porter, and Jerome Kern, to which we learned the lyrics and sang along with the recording.

We were dancing to the music of "Make Believe."

We could make believe
I love you,
Only make believe
That you love me.

First the man sang, then the girl. They sang in pure musical comedy voices: clear and without tremulo. It was sung hesitantly, in dialogue, with pauses between the phrases, as they discovered how they felt about each other as the song progressed. Helen and I sang along with the recorded voices as we danced slowly to the music. I held her close. She was light in my arms, able to follow me effortlessly in a blend of our two bodies.

She must have been thinking about her husband, who had been away for so long. Too long. I was thinking about any number of girls who were about as inaccessible in *that* way as would be expected back before the sexual revolution allowed experimentation of *that* kind between girls and boys.

While holding her close and crooning the words along with the man on the record, my voice began to croak, as it always did when the music got to me. I stopped singing, but I could not stop something else happening. I knew she could feel it, yet she did not move away. But I did as though I was stuck with a cattle prod. We danced with only our arms and shoulders touching until the record was over, but I could feel the heat inflame my neck and face with a blush that would not go down. I was stricken with shame that this would happen while dancing with, of all people, my Aunt Helen, a grown-up, married, older woman, *and* a mother!

I made some feeble excuse about having to do my homework and left for my room in the attic. I felt banished from civilized society (self-imposed, of course) trying to lose myself in homework I ordinarily tried to get over with. When I was called for dinner several hours later I did not dare look at Aunt Helen for fear of blushing all over again. Mother gave me looks from time to time, wondering why I was being so uncommonly quiet.

"Is everything all right at school?" she asked.

I nodded.

"It isn't report card time again, is it?" she persisted, assuming I had failed at school again.

"No," I answered, sneaking a glance at Aunt Helen when I thought she was not looking.

What I saw was a look of quiet amusement and contentment on her face. Her half-smile told me she was not in the least offended by what had happened. It was as if I had affirmed her worth as a woman who could still be thought of in that way.

I relaxed: She did not consider me a sex fiend after all. It was just one of those times when *love* and *LOVE* get mixed up, and the body is not able to make the distinction.

♦

"There's a Cottage Small by a Waterfall"

In Arlington, the year I lived with Bert and Bill, there were woods and fields nearby where we kids could run around and play. That was where I had my first experience with snow, it being my first winter in New England. It was there I learned to ski. I tried to be better than any of the other kids. When we played the usual kids' games it was the same; I had to excel.

Funny thing, though—when we played Cowboys and Indians, everyone but me wanted to be a cowboy or a cowgirl. I could not see anything so great about being a cowboy. The ones I saw in Texas—and there were a lot of them when I lived there—were only about five feet tall or less, with skin that was this side of black, and who spoke a language I did not understand.

Respectable folks did not associate with cowboys except on the range. They were the ones who slept out in the bunkhouse and used their saddles as pillows when they slept under the stars. They may have been considered romantic to the other kids, but as far as most folks were concerned they were considered trash, loners, drifters, or worse. And I remember they were nowhere near as handsome as Tom Mix or Buck Jones or those other guys we saw on the screen at the Saturday matinee. They were just little-bitty Mexicans who weighed no more than a hundred and twenty pounds. Divinity weighs more than that and she is not even full grown yet.

And I could see little difference between being a good or a bad guy when we played Cops and Robbers. Hiding and not getting caught seemed as much fun as having to go out and capture one of the bad guys. Being the hunter or the hunted was about equal in excitement as far as I was concerned, providing, of course, it was I who won. Winning was the important thing.

We had our fights, much like those in the animal kingdom—like Achilles and Stud, for instance—in which we tested one another's strength to determine which of us was the most dominant. We even tried to find out who could pee the farthest.

Warren Story was one of my playmates. He could lick me, although I never could understand why; I was quicker than he and just as strong. He must have been some kind of bully, now that I think about it. It had to be something like that because I could lick everyone else, some of whom could lick Warren. Swiftness and strength are not always what determine domination of one person over another.

Even caring about someone and wanting her to care about you is like finding out who can pee the farthest. I wish it were not so, but that is the way it seems to be.

For instance, there was this girl who lived in the flat below us. She was smarter than the rest of us. I used to hear her practicing her scales on the piano, and after practicing them she would play a song, popular at the time, that began, "There's a Cottage Small by a Waterfall." Missing my mother and sister, and without a father to complete the picture of the ideal family, I pictured myself playing "house" with this pretty girl in that cottage by the waterfall.

I liked Errol a lot. We all did. Warren acted as if she was his girl, but I never saw him try to make any kind of claim on her when she was around any more than the rest of us did. There was no playing "doctor" with her. Without anything being said, we knew what her answer would be. We were also afraid she would haul off and whack us one. She must have gotten some good advice from someone who knew what boys had on their minds where girls were concerned.

We considered her one of us, and we never got into a fight with her if we could help it. She had a sharp tongue and she knew how to use it. Like a fist. She had all us boys beat before we dared lift a hand to her. Even Warren. Errol was a boy's name, like Marion and Carroll. The way she acted around us you would think she was trying to live up to her name.

When I say I liked her, I guess I mean I wanted her to like me, to accept me, to love me.

One time on the front porch we were sitting on the swing. It was one of those that had padded cushions with the same floral design as the cover overhead that was supposed to keep the sun off when you tilted it. I do not remember what I said, but I must have given her some kind of message of how I felt about her, because she said as a kind of warning, "I'm not your girl."

I did not think I had been all that obvious, but I was never any good at hiding things from people. They can read me like a book. Somehow I did not feel rejected by her, though. I accepted it because I knew she was no one else's girl either, especially Warren's.

Freud would say that I had sexual feelings for her, rudimentary though they were, but I was not conscious of them at the time. As far as I knew I just felt great affection for her, even loved her. (Uppercase, of course.)

After I moved back to rejoin my mother at the end of the school year, I did not meet Errol again until we were both in our early twenties. It was about a year before the war, when those of us who were single and over twenty-one were hoping we would not be drafted. By then I had been in and out of love several times. I suspect she had too.

We met on the streetcar. We recognized each other immediately. She was still attractive, but not as pretty as I had remembered her. I cannot remember what we said because it was all small talk. But I do remember wanting to tell her all about what I had accomplished since we had known each other. There was a lot to tell: First of all, I was no longer a dummy who could not read. Not only that, I had graduated from high school; gone to the New England Conservatory of Music; gotten a scholarship to the Leland Powers School of the Theater; played summer stock at the Woodbound Theater in East Jaffrey, New Hampshire; become a vocalist for local dance bands; and was well on my way to making a name for myself in the entertainment world. But I never got to tell her all these things because my stop came up and I had to get off.

When we said good-bye she had a disappointed look on her face. It was a look that told me she was not going steady with anyone at the time, that perhaps her dates were few and far between. I doubt it would have made any difference to her even if I had told her all the things I wanted to tell her to impress her. I think she would have accepted me as I was, as she had remembered me, even as a dumb kid, warts and all.

We said we would have to get together sometime. But we never did. I was drafted into the army several months later, and we were never to be young again.

MOUNTAIN LION

Some sheep breeders try to produce sheep that are about the size of ponies, whereas others strive for beauty; they want their sheep to have straight front legs, a full rump, and a noble bearing that will win prizes at the fair that will get a top price for them. I try for those features too, but I also try for something else—multiple births. I figure twins are worth more than a single, even if it is the handsomest one you ever saw and wins a top prize at the fair. With twins you get four legs of lamb instead of two, if you get my reasoning. (Front legs are called shoulders, not legs, of lamb.) And furthermore, a twin will more likely produce twin offspring. Genetics again.

This year, out of the ten ewes that have produced so far, I have gotten nineteen lambs. That is almost two hundred percent. They have all been normal births. It has been my best year as far as percentages are concerned. The only trouble is, I have lost ten of them to a predator—more than a fifty percent loss.

Last year and the year before that I lost only three. I figured three a year was not so bad, feeling the way I do about such things. But this year, after the loss of our sixth lamb in two weeks, we began to get worried, and my thinking about preserving the balance of nature underwent a change. I called the Wilsons. I had heard they had lost a number of their sheep too. They had evidence that their predator was a mountain lion. Bob said that he and the hunter from the county had gone out after every kill trying to track the lion down, but so far no luck. He gave me the man's number and suggested I call him. I said I would. But I was still undecided. I did not call.

The next week, however, I lost another lamb, even though I now kept the sheep enclosed in the barn area, never dreaming a predator would dare come that close to the barn. I immediately called the number Bob had given me.

Mike came out right away. He asked if there was a carcass. I told him no. "It only takes the little ones."

He did not say much other than to ask questions to see how I felt about things. "If I set a trap and caught one of your neighbor's dogs, what would you do?" he asked.

Having recently had one of my ewes and one of her twins savaged by a pack of five dogs, I did not hesitate to answer. "I'd shoot it," I said, surprised at the depth of my anger.

But I had doubts that it was a dog or dogs. Whatever it was had never taken any of my larger sheep, as had the lion that got the Wilsons' sheep. I figured it had to be a smaller predator, such as a bobcat or a coyote. I told him as much.

All he said was, "You never can tell." He also said that he was not allowed to set traps for mountain lions. He did set smaller traps near the territorial marks he found. "You better keep your dog in the garage tonight," he added.

The next morning he came back. We inspected the traps. Nothing. We did the same every morning that week. Still no luck. On Thursday, when I made my morning count, I found I was missing another lamb. This time there were tracks in the mud. Big ones the size of my fist. Now there was no doubt. The county hunter removed the traps.

"I hate to suggest this," he said. "But you'd better keep your sheep enclosed in the shed from now on. Wire it right up to the roof to be on the safe side."

I did not have the right kind of wire to do it the way he said, but I took wooden field panels I had on hand and hung them on all the opened sides of the shed.

All this while, whenever the Wilsons lost another sheep, Bob and Mike would spend the night trying to track down the lion. By now they had lost six pregnant ewes. All it did was eat the right shoulder, making a fresh kill each time it got hungry. Whereas I had lost seven lambs by this time and the Wilsons only six, their loss was greater than mine; a ewe carrying twins is a loss of three.

A week or so later Bob called. "We finally got it. The dogs lost the scent a couple of times, but we finally got it! I guess we can all relax for a while . . . until the next one comes along and claims the territory."

I still could not convince myself it was the same lion, so I kept my flock penned up each night as a precaution. But when you have to clean out a messy pen every morning, after a while it colors your reasoning. I would never know if it were the same lion unless I left the sheep out in the open barnyard as I had before. I had to find out. The next morning I was missing another lamb.

I immediately strung a heavy wire mesh from the ground to the roof, except on one side where I left the wooden field panels so I could have access to the barn to haul in feed and hay. Reconstructing what had happened the night before, I figured that the lion must have peered in through the wire where before there had been good paneling. The sheep must have mistrusted the wire as sufficient protection, panicked, and rushed against the one remaining wood panel. The pressure of so many sheep splintered it, and they all poured out into the open. The lion took another lamb.

The lion was getting bolder all the time. A friend of mine, who knows about predators, said it was probably an old lion, missing several teeth, and was no longer fleet enough to chase down a deer. That was why it attacked only my lambs and never the ewes or the ram I was keeping out in the open in his own separate pasture. Consequently, if I kept my lambs penned up, it would be only a matter of time before the lion got hungry enough to start taking pets and even taking children.

By now I had reconciled myself to the inconvenience of having to clean out the mess the ewes and the remaining lambs made until I took them to market and could turn the ewes out with the ram in one of the pastures. When the lambing season began the next November, I would have to start penning them in again to protect the little ones. My joy in raising sheep was beginning to wane.

But something happened I did not expect. Several weeks later I looked out the window from our loft and saw a sight that sickened me.

"Oh, no!" I said.

My wife heard me from the bedroom. "What?"

"That bastard's got Studley."

I heard Louise use a word I did not think she knew. She came in and we stood looking out the window at our magnificent ram, lying on his side in his upper pasture, no more than twenty-five yards from the barn and only a little over a hundred feet from the house. Because it was inside the fence, there was no way the lion could carry a three-hundred-fifty-pound ram away as it had the lambs. It would have to return to feed on it, unless it was like the one that took the Wilsons' ewes.

I had not fired a rifle since World War II, but what had to be done was obvious. I needed help, and here it was Sunday. Mike was probably not available on weekends, but I called his office number anyway, hoping there was an answering service to tell him to call me back. There was no answer.

My next door neighbor is a hunter. But I was not about to ask him to sit up, perhaps all night, waiting for a lion that might not show, and then have to go to work the next morning. I did call him, however, to see if I could borrow a rifle. There was no answer. There was no way I could get the lion that night.

The next morning I rushed to the window to see if the lion had returned during the night to feed. It had. The carcass was completely turned around. I immediately called Mike.

He said he would get in touch with Fish and Game and be right over. He and the man from the department arrived a few hours later. After explaining the sequence of events that had led up to his latest kill, I was issued a license that was good for ten days. They recommended that I position myself on the roof and use buckshot, because from that short a distance I would be less likely to miss. Hah!

I was able to borrow a gun from my neighbor, Myron, who also offered to help. After Bob and Mike left, Myron and I made our plans. Around seven that evening, just as it was getting dark, Myron came back with two guns. He had the shotgun and let me have the rifle. He told me to fire only if he missed or merely winged it and it took off, or worse, if it turned and attacked us. We climbed the ladder to the roof of the barn. I had provided us with pads to lie on. We could not see each other on opposite sides of the roof, so I got a length of twine with which we could signal each other by pulling on it.

After about fifteen minutes of waiting, he said, "This is no good. It can see us up here. We better hide in the shed." We climbed down off the roof and positioned ourselves inside the shed on the other side of the barn from where the sheep were penned. Myron was seated to the left, nearest to the shed entrance, with me back and to the right, both in the shadows. If the lion came from the left I would see it first, but I made a vow to myself not to say anything if I saw it before Myron did.

We could not have asked for more ideal conditions. The moon was one night away from being full; there was not a cloud in the sky; the weather was mild; there was no breeze to carry our scent to alert the lion; and the sheep made enough noise to mask any sound we might inadvertantly make. After about another hour of waiting the sheep became suddenly restless. Myron stood up and raised the gun butt to his shoulder. I did not move but flicked off the safety. We waited. After the sheep quieted, he sat down again.

As we continued to wait, alert to the sounds around us, it was a different world, one few of us take the time to witness. And yet, there it is, right outside the comfort of our homes, always there, waiting to be experienced. It is no wonder so many men endure the discomfort of camping out in the wilderness as long as they can hear the night creatures, each calling for attention, declaring its right to be recognized lest it be forgotten or be passed over in the few hours of life alloted to it.

Myron heard something. The sheep became restless. He stood up. I remained seated. Because it came from the left, I saw it first. First the paw, then its head.

I then did something I vowed I would not do. I whispered, "Here it is!" Luckily the sheep were making so much noise the lion would not have heard me had I spoken aloud.

It stalked out into full view, within a few feet of the carcass of the ram. In the moonlight it looked to be six or more feet long, longer than the ram that lay waiting for its killer to feed on him again. Myron fired. The lion dropped in midstep. Myron fired again, then again and again in rapid succession. Overkill, perhaps, but he was taking no chances. There was no need for me to take a shot.

As he rushed to the entrance to see if there was another lion that had accompanied this one, I went into the barn and flicked on the floodlight. We approached the lion as it lay motionless only a few feet from the ram, its eyes glassy in the light of our flashlights, our guns ready if it were to move. But it was quite dead, never to take another of my lambs.

It was an old lion, as my friend had said it would be. A female, not nearly as long as it had looked in the moonlight.

It had scars all over its face and head, so it must have suffered much in making its living on prey less defenseless than lambs. Over its left eyebrow was what I first thought was a purple brown bubble of blood caused by one of the pellets of buckshot, but on further inspection I discovered it was a blood-engorged tick.

My neighbor went home, taking both guns with him. I returned to the house after turning off all the lights at the barn. Whereas I had been quite warm and comfortable while we sat waiting for the lion to appear, I now felt chilled, even though I was indoors sipping coffee. I took a long hot shower. I still felt chilled.

It was a little after ten. I knew I could not sleep. I turned on the TV for the ten o'clock news and heard a report that that very day a mountain lion had been shot after it attacked a six-year-old girl near San Diego. Even this news did not quite ease the feelings I had about my part in killing our lion. When I went to bed it was hours before my feet grew warm again and I could get to sleep.

Two weeks later neighbors on the other side of the hill sighted a mountain lion near their house, and the Wilsons reported the loss of another sheep, a lamb this time.

A WEED IS A FLOWER IN THE WRONG PLACE

South of the equator seasons are reversed. Here on the West Coast there is a similar reversal, and we often find ourselves celebrating Christmas in weather people on the East Coast would consider more appropriate for Easter. This is caused by a high pressure ridge that hovers, sometimes for weeks, over California around the first of the year, forcing cold fronts from the Pacific to rotate north and east and dump snow on eastern cities to give them a white Christmas and us a green one.

Occasionally, when this high pressure ridge breaks down and a cold front from the Gulf of Alaska brings in a couple of inches of snow to alight on us and crown the tops of the surrounding mountains, it reminds me of Christmases in New England when I was young. But snow is rare here, perhaps twice a year, and it stays on the ground only until noon. More often, the front moves in furiously and brings us rain instead of snow, sometimes in torrents, loosening the earth on the slopes, causing floods, mud slides, and considerable damage. On our side, the north, the slopes are densely covered with oaks, buckeye, madrone, and laurel, the deep roots of which keep the topsoil from sliding down into an already fertile valley below.

Appropriately, around Christmas most of our lambs are born. They are born black. But about the time the earth celebrates the real Easter with a burst of wild flowers, the lambs' fleece turns not as white as snow (as in the nursery rhyme) but a dull gray, like their mother's and father's; and light from the warming sun filters through to the floor of our forested slopes, casting shadows to mute the vividness of color so as not to overwhelm the senses.

Spring for us is when the lupin hangs out blue lanternlike flowers topped with white to signal that the rains are about over and the green grass, on which the sheep and the deer have grazed and grown fat, will soon turn rust color and then to gold in the burning sun. Before the lupin turned to flower, the sheep would feast on it. But no more; it is toxic to them now, portending what is to come.

For us, the sorrow of Good Friday comes after Passover and Easter and not before, as is traditional; it is the time for death, when there will be dry grass only, when the lupin will have withered and died, and decisions must be made about which of our lambs must die.

It is simple: If a lamb is not a twin, if it has not grown to considerable size in the shortest possible time, if it is not handsome in some predetermined, genetic sense, its fate is sealed. There is no room for sentiment here. Only the most perfect lambs are saved in order that the breed's most desirable characteristics are perpetuated. The survival of the fattest.

Still, the value we place on things is subjective. For instance, after the war, when Louise and I moved out of our apartment into our first home in a suburb of Los Angeles, our friends gave us gifts of plants and cuttings from their own gardens. We planted them here and there, with little knowledge of what they would grow into. We figured we could leave them if they fitted in, and transplant those that did not.

Amongst all this, one plant appeared and produced an exquisitely fragile, light blue, trumpet-shaped flower, most likely an exotic member of the lily family. Neither of us had ever seen a flower quite like it before, and we could not find it in our search through reference books at the library. We assumed that because it bloomed only at night and closed up during daylight hours it was not a popular flower and therefore not worth listing.

I would take guests out with a flashlight and proudly show off this most rare of flowers and ask if he or she knew what it was. No one did. One smartass suggested we call it a night-blooming jazzman, which is what we did until a more knowledgeable friend said, "Man, that's no flower; that's a goddamn weed!" Somehow, learning that it was a weed did not lessen its beauty for Louise and me. I felt somewhat vindicated years later when I heard a horticulturist say, "There's no such thing as a weed, only a flower in the wrong place."

The husbandman of livestock cannot think this way, however, otherwise he could not do what I had to do today and feel comfortable about it: I took two ewes to be sold at auction. One was the one that had been ruined by a pack of my neighbor's dogs and could no longer be used as a breed ewe. The other was Angel. I had to get rid of her because she developed a bulge about the size of a baseball on her right side. I asked the Wilsons what might be causing it. It could be any number of things, I was told: "a cyst, tumor, boil, a hernia; it could even be a foxtail that's become imbedded and caused an abscess."

"What do you suggest?"

"It's either the vet or the auction."

I knew from experience that a vet would charge more to treat her than both sheep were worth. (As it turned out, I only got forty bucks for both of them.) Consequently, the other side of preserving things of value is deciding when to cut your losses if you are left with no other choice. You can keep cultivating a weed until it turns into a lovely flower because there is little out-of-pocket expense, but the cost of feeding a sheep is much greater than merely watering a weed. When you are a breeder of livestock you become quite callous about such things. It goes with the job.

♦

"In Death There Is Life"

When you are growing up you do not give much thought to the enigmas, paradoxes, and outright contradictions embedded in our most cherished beliefs, faith, and prejudices. We rarely question the myths that support them because we tend to trust what grown-ups teach us. At a young age, most of us are still unable to separate truth from falsehood, and we assume adults know what they are talking about. Thus we take the easy way and let life flow, which it seems able to do whether we know the truth or not. But while we drift, even though we try to forget and bury them from conscious thought, painful memories have a way of filtering through an intentionally obscured screen of time.

During my last year at Hillside School I was put in charge of the dairy. I was doing man's work at the age of twelve, the same age my Uncle Henningson was when he went to sea as an apprentice seaman.

In addition to our regularly assigned chores, we helped out with other things that needed to be done when the seasons demanded it. We cut ice when the pond froze thick enough. We hauled it by pung pulled by a team of horses over slick, snow-laden roads to the ice house, where these hundred-pound blocks of ice were covered with sawdust to insulate them through the spring, summer, and fall until the next winter, when the pond froze over again and the whole process was repeated.

In spring, we helped with the planting. And those of us, who were well behaved and had proven ourselves capable, were invited to stay over the summer to help with work that had to be done to keep the farm operating while school was not in session. Those of us who were selected considered ourselves the elite. We pitched hay, cultivated the crops, and canned the summer vegetables.

But in the fall, when school resumed, we all pitched in and picked apples, shucked corn for the crib, and filled the silo with cut-up cornstalks for fodder for the cows. The most perfect ears of corn were kept for seed. Kernels that came from the straightest rows would produce more perfect corn when they were planted and harvested the following year, we were told. And thus we learned about inherited traits that are passed down from one generation to the next. We were being taught the theories of Darwinism and genetic engineering without knowing what they were called.

But we were also learning that living things, no matter how perfect they are in themselves, sometimes have to be sacrificed for the survival needs of others. "In death there is life."

One time there was a piglet that was to be slaughtered. It had to be caught first. Three or four of us older boys got into the pen and chased after this short-legged, tight little tube of squirming sleekness. Unmindful of the ultimate fate of the victim of our pursuit, we had great fun, chasing it this way and that, trying to head it off without it slipping through our arms and legs. Just when one of us thought he had caught it, it would squeal as if its throat had been cut and would squirm out of his grasp.

Finally, after many unsuccessful attempts, much laughter, and the special delight boys have wallowing around in the dirt, I managed to tackle the pig and hold on to it by lying on top of it until other hands grabbed its legs and we were able to tie it up. Whereupon Pop Sanford cut its throat and its heart went on doing what it was meant to do and pumped all life out of it. It was then slung from a teepeed A-frame by block and tackle and plunged into a cauldron of scalding water to loosen its needlelike bristles so that we could scrape them off. Some of the boys stayed around while it was being butchered. I left.

That night, before I finally got to sleep, I could not get it out of my mind. I almost wept when I considered the part I had in it. Years before I had stepped on a bird and killed it. But that was an accident, therefore forgivable. But this! I had deliberately participated in the piglet's death and enjoyed the fun of its capture; I had even gloried in being the one who did. The next day I traded my portion of meat with the kid next to me for his vegetables, but after a couple of meals, because I preferred meat over vegetables, I turned back to being an omnivore.

♦

Separation

I once heard someone explain that he was a vegetarian because he considered it unchristian to eat meat. For a moment it gave me pause for I, too, felt that being Christian meant that one affirmed the sanctity of *all* living things. I struggled with this for a time because I had always found it hard to reconcile myself to that part of the cosmic scheme of things that makes it necessary for one creature after another in the food chain to die so that the victor might live. Then, I thought to myself, if all this were so, why did Jesus say: "Take. Eat. This is my body; this is my blood. Do this in remembrance of me?"

One of the things that helps me believe in a merciful God is that victims of a predator go immediately into shock. Enkephalins (nature's painkillers) are released into the nervous system to numb the pain. Science tells us that certain other chemicals are released to give the victim of trauma a moment of euphoria before it passes out. These are called endorphins.

But what about separation? I have seen people go into a state of shock when they suffer the loss of someone they love; so severe is their grief they become catatonic. When a lamb is taken from its mother the survivor suffers too. This year, when so many of my lambs were taken by the mountain lion, the day following the attack the mother ewe called out in anguish over the loss of her little one.

Today, I took the two ewes to auction, and since their lambs would thus be weaned, I decided I might as well separate the rest of the lambs from their mothers because all of them are over three months old, which is when I am supposed to wean them anyway. All the lambs and their mothers are out there right now baaing away like mad, showing their displeasure over being separated. It will be a noisy night. It will probably be a couple of days before all the hurt is gone, and they become reconciled to the fact they will never again be reunited.

People, however—the lucky ones—are blessed with faith. It is quite possible that faith (call it what you will) can trigger in the believer a flow of something—perhaps endorphins, or some such chemical not yet identified—to produce hope. We know that hope can alleviate the pain that separation brings. It causes some people to believe that separation from the ones they love will not last. I do not know about sheep.

GUARD DOG

After we shot the lion, none of the folks who feel strongly about the killing of predators came out and told me in so many words that I had done the wrong thing. People are more subtle than that. You can tell by their silence or lack of enthusiasm how they feel. A lady who lives nearby left a folder in my mailbox filled with numerous clippings and photostats of articles she had compiled over the years that told about the usefulness of guard dogs in protecting sheep and other livestock.

Actually I had been thinking about a guard dog since I had lost my first lamb years before, and I was grateful to her for her interest. Her file was voluminous. She even had the phone number of a woman who raised Great Pyrenees.

A Great Pyrenees tends to be a huge dog, about the size of a St. Bernard, with long white hair. It is supposed to be of a gentle nature unless the sheep it is assigned to protect are threatened, and then it will attack the trespasser rather savagely.

I phoned the lady and talked to her a long time, picking her mind about the advantages and disadvantages of having such a dog. She was most generous with her information. What impressed me most about her was her candor. I felt I was dealing with an honest person and one who was enthusiastic about the breed. She said she did not have a young dog at the time but she could sell me a five-year-old male. She had just gotten him back from a woman she had sold him to several years before. Apparently, the woman had kept sheep, was a writer, and had just recently divorced and could no longer keep him.

Usually a young Great Pyrenees with all the proper papers will sell for four hundred dollars on up. "But you can have this one for two hundred," she said. I told her I was interested.

Several years ago our daughter and her family moved to Redwood Valley just outside Ukiah, located about sixty miles north of where the dog was. We decided when next we visited them we could see the dog on our way, and if we wanted to purchase him we could pick him up on our way home.

I did extensive research on the kind of dog the Great Pyrenees was. The file my neighbor gave me was helpful. Other people sent me articles that added to my knowledge, and the more I read the more enthusiastic I became, composing all sorts of pleasant scenarios in my mind about how it would behave with the sheep, Maxie, and me—but, most important, how it would behave toward a predator.

What interested me most about the breed is that it does not necessarily attack a predator if one comes near; it merely stands its ground between it and the sheep it is protecting. Apparently, its size and fearlessness is enough to make a predator hesitate before attacking. There is a lot of hair about the head of the dog that makes it look larger than it is. To a predator it probably looks about the size a polar bear does to us. The lion calculates his chances. His survival depends on his being fleet of foot; if he got hurt in his tangle with the guard dog, perhaps a broken leg, even if he won, he would die of starvation. Therefore, he figures he had better walk away from this one and take his chances on less formidable game, like a lame, old, or sickly deer—or go someplace where there are sheep but no guard dog.

Although I had been told earlier that "with two dogs you only got half a dog," I began to convince myself that if I got another dog a Great Pyrenees was exactly the kind I wanted, especially after I had seen a young one owned by the people we buy our pigs from. Theirs is the friendliest, most lovable clown you could imagine. You would swear it had a perpetual smile on its face as it galomped around playing with Maxie.

When the time came for us to go north to visit the kids, we made arrangements to have a look at the dog, whose name was Beau. The owner and her husband have a big ranch somewhere between Santa Rosa and Petaluma. We followed directions and arrived a little before noon, having driven about four hours from where we live.

No one seemed to be home when we got there. The barn was on the other side of the road from the main house. There were sheep both in the barn and in the shadows of the open shed attached to it. And in among the sheep sat Beau, a most magnificent beast if there ever was one.

I got out of the car and approached the fence that surrounded the barn area. I was not foolish enough to open the gate and go in. Presently Beau came toward where I was standing. He did not come in a rush to greet me with tail wagging and a smile on his face treating me as a long-lost friend. He appeared to be tethered. Attached to his collar was a chain about twenty feet long. And when Beau approached where I stood behind the fence, I then saw why he came so slowly; the chain was attached to a tire he dragged behind him.

Because Beau did not know me, I saw an opportunity to determine if he was, indeed, a good guard dog. I stood my ground, somewhat reassured after I saw he was tethered to an automobile tire, and waited for him to get near the fence behind which I stood. He approached me steadily. When he got to his side of the fence, all the while looking me in the eye, I said, "Hello, Beau," in a nice friendly voice.

Now I must say that from somewhere in the lower depths of Beau came a sound as from some beast four times as big as he, whose size was impressive enough as it was. It was not a dog's bark. It was a growl like the sound Godzilla made in the movie of the same name. But I held my ground. With Beau tethered to a tire, and thus encumbered, I knew that if he made a threatening move toward me, I could be back in the car before he could get to me.

About that time the owner came from the main house

and approached us from across the street, making friendly welcoming sounds that immediately put Beau at ease. After introductions were made all around, she said that she could not let me have the dog until the next day because that was when Beau's quarantine would be lifted.

"Quarantine?"

She explained that the sheriff had put Beau on quarantine because he had recently attacked a boy.

I said, "What!"

She further explained that it was not Beau's fault. The boy had been teasing him and Beau really had not done all that much harm; he just bit him on the shoulder. "But his teeth didn't puncture the skin," she added reassuringly. "It was just a warning bite."

Now if she had said Beau had bitten him somewhere lower—say, on his leg—it would not have sounded so bad. But on his *shoulder*! It gives some idea how big this breed of dog is.

Then this woman did a very brave thing. She opened the gate, went in and stroked Beau's head. He immediately turned to mush and lay over on his side exposing his belly to be rubbed. He was as gentle under her touch as Maxie is to mine.

She then told me to stroke Beau. I did. He responded

with a most benign and loving look to show me I was no longer a potential enemy now that his mistress had made it known I was a friend. I immediately fell in love with this big polar bear of a dog.

She told Beau to get up. She unhooked the chain from his collar and attached a shorter lead, and walked away with the dog obediently following her. She said, "Heel." Beau followed a step or two behind her. She stopped. Beau stopped.

She told me to take the lead. I did. I led him away, saying, "Heel," which he did. He stopped when I did and followed when I resumed walking. I was gaining confidence by the minute.

"As you can see, Beau is a well-behaved dog," she said. "He responds well to orders."

But I was thinking, Why then is he chained to a tire?

She must have read my mind because she said, "Beau has a habit of jumping the fence and running away from time to time. That's why he's chained to the tire for now."

I said, "What!"

"I suggest you keep him chained to a tire for about two months until he gets used to his new surroundings."

I nodded, for I knew I would stammer had I attempted to speak.

Then she volunteered the following information: "This breed's not been bred to be a herding dog like your Border collie. It's bred to be a guard dog only, therefore I suggest you keep Beau at the barn at all times. Never take him with you when you take the flock out to graze. If you do, whenever your dog tries to herd the sheep, Beau will think your dog is attacking them and will do what he's been trained to do and attack. Oh, yes, and another thing—when you turn the ram in with the ewes, whenever the ram tries to mount one of them, Beau will go after the ram, thinking it's attacking the ewe."

Several questions came to mind, but before I could ask any of them she continued. "Because of the way Beau has been mistreated by the husband of his former owner, he doesn't take very kindly to men. I don't know for sure, but I suspect the man was growing pot and, in addition to guarding the sheep, Beau was also trained to guard their crop. The former owners were getting a divorce and were often away, leaving Beau to take care of things. When I got Beau he was quite rundown and had suffered a great loss of weight. He hasn't got it all back yet, as you can see."

She showed me his ribs, which were quite visible. "It'll take another month or so before Beau regains all his strength and is his old self again."

I thought about the cost of Beau's feed bill, but before I

broached that subject I asked if there was anything else I should know.

"Well, yes," she went on, "this breed has a tendency to get ear mites. You'll have to put Mitox in his ears every ten days or so. He doesn't like his ears fooled around with, though, so you'll have to tie a muzzle around his mouth when you put drops in his ears. And it's a good idea to keep Beau's hair clipped short to keep him from getting foxtails. They become embedded if you're not careful. You can see on his belly"—she showed me—"where he's recovering from the infection he had when I got him back. Beau's been terribly neglected, as you can see."

"What about food?" I asked finally.

"I usually have two large bowls of food on hand. I better warn you, though: Never take a bowl away from him, even an empty one, or he'll snap at you. I always have another full bowl to give him at the instant I take the empty bowl away."

Now you would think by this time I would be discouraged. Instead, I somehow saw all this as some kind of challenge. One who is born with a handicap and overcomes it has a tendency to invite challenges or, when confronted with one, meets it head-on. Therefore, I promised to return in a couple of days when, after visiting the kids, we would pick Beau up and take him home with us.

Driving to Redwood Valley, Louise was strangely quiet. Ordinarily she talks a lot, but when she does not, it does not necessarily mean she is not thinking.

Finally, she said in that quiet way of hers that tells me she has got something on her mind I should give my most serious attention to, "Do you really think you should get this dog?"

"I've been thinking about it."

"Do you think it's wise?"

"How do you mean?"

"I was thinking of Maxie. Won't she be jealous?"

"Perhaps. At first. But you know Maxie. She's the friendliest dog there is. What's more, boy and girl dogs usually get on fine; it's when they're the same sex there's a problem. Anyway, Beau'd be at the barn all the time with the sheep. Maxie never leaves the area around the house unless she's with me. You know that."

"What about when Maxie is herding the sheep?"

"I wouldn't take Beau with us. I'd lock him up in the barn."

"What about Beau jumping the fence and taking off?"

"Like the lady said, I'll have to keep Beau chained to a tire for a couple of months."

"But what about when we go away," she persisted in that quiet and determined way of hers, "when we have to get someone to take care of the sheep? Won't that be a problem?"

"Yeah," I admitted reluctantly, for I still felt intrigued by the challenge, not quite willing to give up on Beau yet.

Wisely, Louise did not pursue it further. She let me go on thinking about it, which she has found over the years is the best way to handle decisions such as this; and which, when I think about it, is probably the way most decisions are made in our household, as perhaps it is in others. By the time we got to Redwood Valley, however, my mind was made up.

While I was talking with our son-in-law, our daughter, Christine, casually asked Louise about the dog. I saw out of the corner of my eye Louise indicate with a shake of her head that now was not a good time to bring the subject up for she had planted the seed of doubt in my mind as to the wisdom of getting the dog. Christine immediately clammed up. I pretended not to have witnessed the byplay between them—I would play along just long enough to heighten the tension. I was hesitating because I dreaded having to tell the woman, who had been so nice and honest about disclosing the possible difficulties I might have with Beau, that I would have to renege on my promise to her.

Finally, after playing the delaying game long enough, I asked Christine for a telephone book to find the woman's number. (The fact that she volunteered to look the number up gave some idea of how eager she was to help her mother's cause along.)

With the right amount of regret in my voice I told the woman that, all things considered—not the least of which was my fear of Beau's unpredictability, his possible attack on the ram, my dog, the neighbors, and just about anybody else who came within a mile of our property, including me—it would be better for me not to have another dog at this time, especially Beau. I hastened to add that I would gladly send her a check to cover any inconvenience I may have caused her.

She was very understanding and said for me to forget the check, that perhaps I might consider buying a younger dog when she had one available and could give it the right training to suit my needs. I said I sure would consider it and, after I thanked her, I hung up, relieved I had gotten out of it so easily.

On the drive back home, Louise was her talkative self again, except for the few minutes it took to pass by Santa Rosa. We both were silent in deference to Beau, whom we knew was a most lovable dog and one we would have taken into our hearts readily had he not been so good at the job he was bred and trained to do.

THE LOTTERY

The thinking behind having a guard dog like Beau to make a predator hesitate before attacking our lambs brings to mind what Churchill said about Hitler back in the mid-thirties. He said that he should be stopped before it was too late. Hitler was not challenged; he got bolder, and before long the whole world was at war.

But back then, like millions of other boys, I could not have cared less that our nation's cause was honorable, or that our mobilizing for war kept a bully like Hitler from further aggression against his weaker neighbors. A couple of years before we got into it, Hitler was the least of my worries. He was way over there. I wanted to delay having to prove myself less a coward than the next guy for as long as possible.

Back in 1940, Congress passed a law that was euphemistically called the "Selective Service Act," which meant that all men would be drafted into the army who were over twenty-one, not married, or were othewise unfit for combat training because of health reasons. There was to be a lottery, and those whose numbers were drawn first had to go first.

I had a selfish reason for not wanting to be called. I was pursuing a rather promising career in the theater.

After high school I attended the New England Conservatory of Music, but because I was as poor a "sight reader" of music as I was of the written word, it was obvious I would never become even an adequate musician. I had my father's talents but not his musicianship. I became a vocalist with dance bands in and around Boston, however, crooning the sentimental love ballads of the time; and later I got a scholarship at the Leland Powers School of the Theater. I also got a job playing summer stock at the Woodbound Theater in East Jaffrey, New Hampshire.

Therefore, you could say that one of the main reasons I

did not want to be drafted was that I still could not read well aloud. Not only would induction have interrupted my budding career, but all my contacts would be lost by the time I got out, and I would have to start all over again reading scripts cold at auditions, something I did very poorly.

Mother, as always, was trying to make things easier for me. She felt protective, as I suppose all mothers feel toward an only son, especially if he has been orphaned at an early age. She had me talk to Dr. Cutler, who had been in the service during the First World War. He said I should do everything possible to stay out of the draft. (I could not have agreed with him more.)

"I was in for the whole eighteen months during the last one," he said. "If I had to do it over again, I would go back to school, get married, or take a job that was essential to the war effort to keep out of it." (He got no argument from me.)

A week or so later, a friend of the family who knew someone connected with a firm that made aircraft parts, suggested I apply for a job, and, as though I did not know why, I was hired, even though I had never done that kind of work before.

I was assigned to a rotary grinding machine, cutting grooves into cylinders that were used somewhere in Pratt &

Whitney aircraft engines. It took no intelligence whatever. And after I proved I had the skill to do this kind of precision work, I found it was the most boring job I had ever had to do.

To make matters worse, I was the only one who worked the swing shift, probably isolated from the others because I was someone for whom a job was made.

I was told to finish a minimum number of cylinders on each shift. But there was no one around to tip me off that if I made more than the minimum I would force the quota up, making it tougher for those who were too slow to keep pace. How was I to know that by doing my best, which Hillside school had taught me was how you hung on to a job, I was turning into a hated quota buster? Hillside did not teach me about unions.

After a thirty-day probationary period I was expected to join the union if I proved myself skilled enough. I would then be considered someone essential to the defense of my country and thereafter would be exempted from the draft.

Those on the day shift had other ideas, however. During their shift they exchanged some of their out-of-tolerance cylinders with mine, which made it look like half of mine were rejects.

When the foreman confronted me about it, I told him

there must be a mistake. He looked at me as though he doubted me. I told him that thereafter I would put my finished cylinders in a separate box, hide it in his office, and he could examine the cylinders each morning before the others got there. I did.

The next time we met he acknowledged that my grooves were well within the required tolerance, but that perhaps I should keep closer to the quota already established by the day shift. Obviously, he was implying more than he was saying, making me realize I was not cut out for this sort of work. Doing a job in the slowest possible way with a "so we don't work ourselves out of a job" attitude made me want to let myself get drafted when my number came up. It was supposed to be for only one year anyway, and by now I figured I might as well get it over with so I could get on with a career that was less boring than operating a rotary grinding machine, especially for a hyper kid like me who had always had difficulty slowing down to the pace of others.

And it probably would have been for that one year if only we had heeded Churchill's warning about Hitler.

(It reminds me of what a friend of mine said shortly after I reported the first kill the lion made on one of my lambs. He said I should stake out another lamb on a moonlit night and wait for the lion to come after it. If I had followed his suggestion when he first made it, I would have saved the lives of all those other lambs. Not only that, I ended up killing the lion anyway.)

I knew someone on the draft board—not high up, but someone who knew where to look to find out the information I needed. He said my number was coming up in another couple of months, and if I waited I would be sent to Fort Bragg in North Carolina. But if I went with the next bunch to be drafted I would be among the last to be sent to Camp Edwards on Cape Cod, about sixty miles from home. Now I have nothing against North Carolina, but the Cape was nearer home, therefore I became a kind of hero, a patriot—I volunteered. This was a year before Pearl Harbor.

I was inducted into the 26th Division, called the Yankee Division. We were told it had acquitted itself rather honorably against Germany during the First World War, doing its part "to make the world safe for democracy."

And once in, I began to hope that mobilizing for war the way our nation was would be enough to make a bully like Hitler back off, and I would, indeed, be in for that one year only.

◆

Zeus the Goose

Recently, a young couple who lived on the other side of our mountain had to move to the city. They had a duck and a goose they could not take with them. Because we have a stock pond, they asked if I would take them.

The man must have heard about our lion problem and why I hesitated, because he then explained that at first they also had had several laying hens.

"Even though we enclosed them in a fenced-in chicken coop, we lost them all except for the duck and the goose."

"How do you figure that?"

"I don't know," he said. "Maybe waterfowl have ways of protecting themselves that chickens don't."

Now waterfowl are the oddest-looking creatures you will ever see when they waddle around on solid ground, since it is not their natural element, and you would think the duck and goose would take to the pond like the proverbial duck does to water, but when I put them into the fenced area around our stock pond, they virtually had to learn to swim.

Louise named the goose Zeus. According to Greek mythology, Zeus turns into a swan and mates with Leda, which could not happen here, so instead of naming the duck Leda, she named her Sally. Sally's full name is Sally Forth because "she's the first to take to the pond." But once Zeus the goose learned to swim and finally ventured beyond a few feet from shore, he looked as serene as the majestic white swan he was named after.

Sally pays little attention to the sheep, spending most of her time swimming around on the pond, frequently baring her feathered butt for all the world to see as she searches the pond floor for food. Zeus seems more interested in the sheep.

The first time he saw one he reached out his neck (as we might extend an arm to feel something with our fingers we've never felt before) and took an exploratory peck at the sheep's behind. All he got was a beak full of wool. The ewe did not even notice. Bewildered by her lack of response, Zeus became even more curious and tried intimidation to see what this strange creature's reaction might be.

A goose can be quite formidable when it attacks, pounding relentlessly with its flapping wings. Zeus flailed at the ewe, but, fortunately, his wings struck harmlessly against the ewe's fleece-cushioned flanks. She merely lowered her head, butted Zeus away, and went on grazing. Sheep, and most other creatures except the human animal, do not nurse anger for long and go nonchalantly about their business until threatened again.

Undaunted, Zeus stretched out his long neck an inch or two above the ground (looking like a miniature brontosaurus might have looked if it had feathers) and made a frontal attack. But the ewe again met the challenge, its forehead being a sheep's most unvulnerable spot, and swept Zeus away as she had the first time. Zeus backpedaled awkwardly on his orange-colored webbed feet, decided he had met his match and thereafter left the older sheep alone. He backed down, as all bullies do when challenged, and started intimidating the lambs instead.

Now, when Zeus is not in the pond swimming around with Sally, he is usually with the lambs; and when he is not acting toward them like a teacher who has learned how to get a class of unruly pupils to behave by peering at them with an imperious look that dares them to challenge his authority, he honks at them like some haughty drill sergeant barking out orders to keep a platoon of recruits in line. At first, we thought Zeus was asserting his authority over the lambs in order to satisfy his need to command; it was not until later that we discovered there was also a more touching reason.

We still had not killed the lion, and the first few times I went down to the barn at night to investigate the reasons for Zeus's alarmed honking, I could not tell if he had been squawking at the lion when it came into the barn area to make its kills or was scolding the lambs just to be bossy. Sometimes, after I responded to Zeus's alarms, I saw the lion's footprints and sometimes not. Therefore, Zeus as sentinel was not to be trusted; he had cried wolf too often. Strange thing though: After I penned the flock up in the shed, the lion never bothered the duck or the goose as far as I could tell. Either they swam to the middle of the pond and the lion could not follow, or Zeus came at the lion with such a fury of honks and flapping outspread wings that all the lion got was a bruised head or a tasteless mouthful of feathers and went elsewhere in search of easier game. I never saw its footprints anywhere near the pond. They always came from the opposite direction.

It was not until after we shot the lion and all but three of the littlest lambs were sent to market that Louise noticed something. "The way Zeus is behaving, you'd think those lambs are his sole responsibility."

"You know, I think you're right," I answered.

Because we sell only our larger lambs, keeping the slower-growing ones for our own freezer, this year when the hit man came to put down the remaining lambs the older sheep took off and huddled in the remotest corner of the pasture, because animals can sense death. Maxie hid in the garage. But Zeus stayed with the three little ones, as though his presence would prevent what he knew was about to happen. When the first one was shot, however, he found there was little he could do about it; he could only cry out in anguish.

You would think by now I had become inured to the inevitability of what happens to every creature that is sacrificed so that others may live. But the hurt in Zeus's cry was more than I could take. I immediately left the killing grounds to let the man do what he was paid to do and, like Maxie, protected myself less from witnessing the slaughter of the lambs than from hearing Zeus's outcry of grief.

I found myself wondering how the man who did the killing felt about it. I knew that somewhere along the line he had had to come to terms with his feelings about being a killer—for how else could he endure what he had to do each day? I suppose he reasons, as perhaps we all would if we had no choice, that "someone's got to do it," but I have yet to hear him, or any other hit man we have had up here, say he enjoyed it.

It is even worse for a combat soldier. Even knowing he is only doing his duty and can say in all truthfulness, "I'm only following orders," he has to come to terms with what he does. I did.

Therefore, I fully understand why people feel so strongly

against their participation in any phase of killing (such as war), and why some would rather go to jail and suffer the scorn of their fellow man than bear arms. There are those who go so far as to offer no resistance and "turn the other cheek" even if it means they will be killed when they do. That takes a special kind of courage, perhaps even a greater courage than he who follows orders to "kill or be killed," like I had to do.

♦

Colonel Kirk's Jerks

My regiment was the "Old One Hundred and First," which could trace its origin all the way back to the Revolutionary War. Naturally, we identified with the "minute men" at Lexington and Concord; our regiment had helped gain our nation its independence. Soldiers whose own regiments could not claim such a famous history referred to ours as the "Old Hundred and Worst," and because our commanding officer's name was Kirk, we were also called "Colonel Kirk's Jerks." We merely smirked at our detractors because we knew we were pretty special.

Now I suppose I would be expected to say that this was

one of the roughest times of my life. It was not. After basic training I got to drive a truck, which meant I did not have to walk and do guard duty. I suppose you could say that was typical army logic, because I had never driven a truck before, but I was probably chosen because I had a driver's license and had operated a rotary grinding machine on my last job.

I found that life in the army is rather like I imagine living under a socialist regime would be. If you adopt the right attitude—and I did most of the time—you experience much freedom from worry. If you allow others to think for you, there will always be those who will gladly take over the job. Somewhat like Zeus and the lambs. And it is probably the reason some people find both the army and the welfare state rather appealing: Both he who lusts for power and he who prefers to be led and have someone else do his thinking for him have their needs fulfilled.

But as a basically restless person, I found it difficult to conform to a life that is regimented. And there were others who felt as I. It was not long before some of us found a back road through the woods, that other less motivated people did not find out about, where there was no sentry on guard to stop us from driving off the army reservation without a pass. (This was a year before the war and command was rather lax about these things.) And often, but not enough to attract attention, we would sneak down to the motor pool in the dark of night and with a duplicate key (the same one fit all the trucks) start one and drive it through the back gate all the way to Boston, spend most of the night, and be back before reveille, quite sleepy but happy we could show we could think for ourselves and that we had somehow beat the system.

But do not get me wrong, that first year in the army I usually followed orders and, for the most part, I was a good soldier. In other words, I never got caught bending the rules. As I say, I had the time of my life. But a year later this soldiering business became serious; we were at war, in "for the duration," which meant another four years for those of us lucky enough to survive.

♦

"If We Got Married It Would Spoil Everything"

That was almost fifty years ago, and since then we have had the Korean (called a police action) and the Vietnam Wars —I forget the euphemism for that one—and all those other conflicts that happen in other countries that we close our eyes to because "it's over there, and it doesn't affect us directly."

While Maxie and I are out tending the sheep, I sometimes find myself wondering about people who demonstrate against nuclear weapons and war and what good it does. I am against it, of course. War, I mean. In fact, I do not know anyone, especially someone who has seen it firsthand, who would want another one—any kind of war, nuclear or otherwise.

Back during the Vietnam War, our son, George, was a conscientious objector. Our daughter, Christine, was going with a boy who was also a CO. But their cases were different, perhaps unique. To my knowledge I do not think they marched in antiwar demonstrations, but, at least, they did try to do something about it.

It was back when the sexual revolution was just starting and my generation was having trouble adjusting to what we considered an erosion of our traditional values of home, family, and all that. Chris and Jon lived together, but the reason they gave for not getting married was not necessarily that they did *not* believe in marriage; rather, it was because Jon was not yet twenty-one.

"Hunnh?" I said.

"If we got married it would spoil everything."

It was obvious I was having difficulty understanding what they meant until they explained that Jon's father had been a CO in the Second World War, when it was not popular to be one. He had recently told the authorities that because his son was a minor, he was responsible only to his parents, therefore it was they who should be punished; Jon was only doing what he was told. You can see the spot that put the government in. Think of all the other under-twenty-ones who would escape the draft until they came of age if the argument held up in court. And Jon's parents were willing to take it to the Supreme Court if need be.

Chris and Jon wanted to have a family whether they were married or not, but decided that they had better do their traveling while they were still young and before they got tied down with children. The only trouble was, traveling in Europe and both being under twenty-one, they were warned that their status would be questioned at every hotel and they were likely to be denied lodging. (At that time many people in Europe viewed unmarried teenage kids living and traveling together about as narrowly as I did.)

Finally, in September, after they had lived together as man and wife for about a year, Chris called and said she and Jon wanted to get married. Louise and I were on the next plane. But once they were married the whole scheme about Jon's parents being liable for his refusal to be inducted was made invalid. Now, as a married man, he was considered "head of household," and therefore the whole case was put in question. Jon never did go into the service, nor was he ever put in jail as his father had been during the Second World War; he did alternate service.

With their kind of antiwar background it is understandable why we had been warned never to give Alex, our grandson, any toy guns for Christmas. We complied. They also refused to have a TV in the house because they did not want him exposed to anything that might desensitize him to the harm violence does to people.

Later, a few years before we retired to the Carmel area, Louise and I visited Chris and Jon. Chris was driving us through town. I was in the front seat, Louise in the back with Alex, then about three or four years old.

Alex made a sound. He had extended his index fingers to form the barrel of a gun and, apparently as he had seen the kids in preschool do, with an *a-a-a-a-a* he wiped out half the population of Carmel.

Poor Christine. My heart went out to her, for I saw it was then that she realized, as all concerned parents do, that we cannot always protect our children from the rest of society and its negative influences.

And now, as I sit here writing this, I hear Zeus barking out commands to this year's crop of lambs. I ask myself, Doesn't that dumb goose realize that he has again made himself responsible for their fate?

Soon, as he did last year, he will be crying out in anguish as each little one is taken. And all the while, as she did last year when the killings took place, Sally will duck her head in the water searching for food (apparently unconcerned about what is going on) while Maxie hides in the garage, I in the house, and Zeus acts like he can do something about it.

He probably will again next year too.

"I'VE SEEN IT ALL"

Driving in rural areas, every mile or so one sees vertical metal panels about six inches wide by three feet long lining the backroads. They are painted white and, because they usually have large numbers and letters painted on them, they probably have some purpose other than reflecting light to serve as markers for driving at night.

Years ago, when Louise and I were looking for property where we might build a place to escape to when I retired, we drove a scenic secondary road from Highway 101 toward the coast through Anderson Valley and the majestic redwood groves north of San Francisco. Louise brought my attention to the panels that lined the roads. They had *SON* and *MEN* printed on them in large letters.

Now about that time the Equal Rights Amendment to the constitution was first being ratified by the various states, which, if passed, would guarantee women equality with men, at least constitutionally if not in fact. And probably with this in mind, Louise made some reference to the male chauvinists in the road department who had deliberately put *SON* and *MEN* on these markers only to affirm their masculinity. Of course, *SON* was the abbreviation for Sonoma and *MEN* for Mendocino, the two counties we were passing through.

Those in the forefront of every effort that threatens to upset how we look at things usually take themselves rather more seriously than the rest of us do at the time. Therefore, being on holiday and a little frivolous, Louise and I delighted ourselves in thinking up changes in our language that would have to be made so as not to offend those in the feminist movement.

This was some years ago, so the word game we played

may not seem all that original anymore. For us it was. For instance, girl's choirs would sing from hermnals instead of hymnals, women's skirts would have hermlines instead of hemlines, and a book would be written on the subject entitled *The Herstory of Women*. More to the point, the medical profession would have to think up another name for a hysterectomy. And so on.

Most of us agree that there should be equality of opportunity, but we unconsciously resist change because it means we have to make adjustments. One way of easing ourselves into accepting change is to make light of it, which is probably the reason we played this harmless word game, knowing that change was going take place anyway no matter how we felt about it.

I was talking to Aunt Bertha a couple of years ago a few months before she died at the age of ninety-two. She was the last of them all; my mother had died only a year or so before at the age of ninety-three.

I loved my Aunt Bertha. One of the reasons was because she spent the rest of her life trying to make it up to me for failing as a substitute mother the winter I lived with her and Uncle Bill. But then, in my case, even the Blessed Mother Mary would have been sorely tested. Louise and I were on our way to Europe and stopped by to visit her in Virginia, where she lived with her daughter, Lois. We knew we would never see each other again, and that last morning, before Louise and I drove to the airport for our flight to New York, I sat with Aunt Bertha in her room and visited.

She said, "In my lifetime I've seen it all. I've seen the electric light replace lamps and candles, the automobile replace the horse and carriage, the airplane replace the train as the quickest way to get from one coast to the other. I've lived to see movies, the radio, the talkies, and the atomic bomb. On TV I even saw the first man walk on the moon at the very moment it was happening. But that was only in the field of science. Just think of the social changes that have taken place as well."

She paused and looked at me for a long time. I had been briefly active in the civil rights movement back in the mid-sixties. I guess she needed to let me know how she felt about it.

"I want to show you something," she said, going to get a picture of her third or fourth grade class. "Can you tell which one is me?" she asked, smiling.

I laughed. It was not that she was easily identifiable because she was the only blonde, but because she and a couple of other girls were the only white children in the picture. All the rest were black.

"That's Boston for you," she said proudly. "You know, I had completely forgotten I had gone to school with black children until I found this picture a few years ago," she added, knowing I would understand what she meant.

"I was the first and only one of us to go to college," she continued. "None of the others even got to finish high school. But I never used the education I got to make something of myself. Instead, I got married and became just a housewife and a mother."

It was the *just* that got me. I did not know how to answer her.

"When I was growing up women couldn't vote," she went on. "Not until nineteen twenty. I was twenty-three before I got to vote for the first time." Again she laughed. "And then I went and voted for Warren Harding. In those days a woman's vote merely echoed her husband's." She reminded me of my grandmother at times like these.

She was silent for a time and then added, "Yes, I've seen it all. I wish I'd taken a greater hand in it. I could have. We still have a long way to go—women, I mean—unfortunately, I won't get to see it."

When something does not involve you directly, you are not as likely to pay as much attention to it as perhaps you should. Often we need to have our eyes opened to the changes that are taking place right before our eyes.

◆

It's Been Nice Seeing You

Several years ago, after we had lived here a short time, the men who own the pond across the road from our property were going away for the weekend; and because I usually take a walk a couple of times a day along the road that separates our properties, I was asked to keep an eye out for trespassers, who, when they drive by and see the pond and the view, often stop for a look. You cannot blame them; it is so beautiful. Some visitors, however, take advantage, and treat it like public picnic grounds, which they assume are maintained by the local parks department. Consequently, they leave trash and otherwise destroy its natural beauty.

My daughter and her family were visiting, and my son-in-law, a designer/builder, and I took a stroll over to the other side of the mountain to look at a house that was in the process of being built. We took a shortcut through the pond property. On breaking through the row of evergreens that partially mask the pond from the road, we saw a couple lying on the beach. They had parked their convertible nearby and had the radio on. It was blasting out rock and roll, which made them immediately suspect. As Jon and I approached the couple, and I was thinking of a diplomatic way of saying they were trespassing, we were practically on them before I realized they were not in bathing suits. They were both nude; their oiled bodies gleaming golden in the sun.

I was so surprised my first reaction was to turn around and leave, but I felt it my duty to inform them they were trespassing. Duty first.

Trying to keep my eyes shifting on anything and everything but the girl's body, I politely asked if they knew they were on private property.

The man said, "Yes. We got permission from Jim and Dick to use the pond while they were away."

I was immediately apologetic and said I had been told to keep an eye out for trespassers and did not realize they had gotten permission. We exchanged a few more words, none of which I remember because my mind was on other things, and I left as soon as I could with as much dignity as I could summon.

After inspecting the house we had gone to see in the first place (and got to see more than we expected), Jon and I returned home, but we did not return by way of the pond; we took the long way around. Why?

I doubt it would have bothered Jon as much as it did me to have returned by way of the pond; the young of today are less tense about nudity than my generation. It has to do with the way we were brought up. Since the pill and the more permissive attitudes toward sex, the young of this generation are allowed to do things the young of my generation could only fantasize about.

But I do not feel deprived. When I was growing up I considered girls the most enchanting of all creatures. There was mystery about them. There still is.

I always felt they were so much smarter than I. (But then, boys were too.) What I mean is that girls were so much better in school than boys: They behaved themselves; they were neater about things; they took things much more seriously and were always more sympathetic, tender, and feeling about the important things in life. They did as they were told; they would grow up to be mothers, which was something we boys could never be. In those days being a housewife and a mother was highly regarded and not considered, as my Aunt Bertha said, "*just* a housewife and a mother." As far as I was concerned, girls were superior to boys in just about every department except sports. It is likely that this was because girls had something I wanted, which they had been taught to keep just out of reach, which made them special in a special kind of way.

I find myself asking: "Where, oh, where, is the enchantment that once there was?" But then, for generations younger than mine, they too have experienced at one time the enchantment of not knowing. Perhaps what I think is missing is that innocence, or Victorian prudery—call it what you will—is lost earlier for them than when I was growing up. And perhaps knowing all there is to know, whereby nothing is left to the imagination, the mystery is lost to them forever.

But who am I to say which is preferable? Every generation has its own idea of what is enchanting.

When the owners of the pond returned and I had a chance to talk to Dick, I told him about the two nudes on the beach. We both had a chuckle over it. Laughingly, I said: "At least, I didn't say to the girl as I was leaving, 'Well, it's been nice seeing you.'"

Funny how stories are passed around and become legends: Try as I may to get it straight, the story persists to this day that those were my parting words to the nude girl.

THE BETTER WINES COME FROM GRAPES THAT HAVE BEEN MADE TO SUFFER

Several years ago a neighbor of ours had an oak tree near his house that had become completely stripped of its leaves. He called in a man whose job it is to spray trees that become infested. Playing on my neighbor's fears, the bug man said that if he did not immediately spray it with an insecticide to rid it of these tiny green caterpillars that were eating the leaves, all the surrounding oak trees would become infested too. "It could spread all over the valley," he warned. My neighbor had his tree sprayed.

The following summer I was bulldozing a jeep trail to gain access to our lower acreage and I saw a number of oak trees covered with a blizzard of white butterflies. "They look just like snowflakes," I said to myself. "And in the midst of summer, yet."

I was informed that they were oak moths. And later, to my delight, I saw the same type of butterfly fluttering around several of the trees nearer our house.

A few weeks later I noticed that the century-old oak tree that shadows the front of our house had become covered with little green caterpillars about an inch long that were just like the ones that had attacked my neighbor's tree the year before. And just as the bug man had warned, in a matter of days the whole valley looked like the Demilitarized Zone between North and South Vietnam after it had been defoliated with Agent Orange.

After the worms had stuffed themselves with nearly every green oak leaf in sight, they went into their next stage of development. They became cocoons, encapsulating themselves into white shrouds of silk, attaching themselves to every ceiling, wall, and branch they could find. But now, at least, I consoled myself, they did not fly away or roll and become squishy as they had in their caterpillar stage when I had tried, none too successfully, to sweep them up. I could now brush these lifeless dried husks down from the walls, the ceilings of our barn, and under our decks with a broom, and thus gather dustpans full of them to be burned. I figured that the following year, when those that escaped my efforts had emerged from their cocoons as lovely butterflies and started the whole pestilential process over again, I would have the insecticide man come and kill off those that survived so as to halt another devastating infestation. It was the least I could do toward saving the beauty of our valley. I hoped others would do likewise.

I need not have worried: The following year the oak moths did not return, except for a few that attacked isolated trees as they normally would in other years. The rest of the trees returned into full bloom, their leaves more abundant than before.

I asked around for an explanation. The theory that appealed to me most was the one that claimed that the oaks themselves prevent another infestation by manufacturing a certain chemical that renders oak moths infertile, impeding their progress beyond the cocoon stage. Indeed, when I looked around at those that escaped the reach of my broom the year before, they just hung there like so many white lanterns without the power to light them into wakefulness so they could emerge again as lovely moths. They had died in their sleep, to rest for all eternity in some kind of purgatory, never to earn their wings.

But even more astounding for me after I researched it further, I read that when oaks are thus attacked by enough of these caterpillars, they alert neighboring trees in some way still unknown that it is time to start manufacturing whatever the narcotic is that lulls the pupae into an everlasting sleep.

Someone we know, who can name all the wild flowers and knows about things like this, said several interesting things: "Those moths are nature's pruners. They appear every seven to ten years and benefit our forests the same as an occasional forest fire does.

"In fact," she added, "I think naturally caused forest fires should be left to burn themselves out—unless, of course, they endanger homes."

She got our attention. The year before we moved here the Marble-Cone fire raged uncontrolled for weeks through the wilds of the Las Padres National Forest, threatening to move into the Cachagua Valley, up the south side of our mountain and burn us out. Our house was then under construction, and when we visited on weekends to monitor its progress, we noticed that the whole area was covered with a dusting of ashes that the wind carried over from the fire to settle over everything like dirty snow.

"You can water an oak tree too much and kill it," she continued in her knowing way. "Trees and flowers, just like people and animals, must be made to suffer in order for them to thrive best. They become subject to all sorts of diseases that will eventually kill them if you don't allow them an opportunity to build up their own natural resistances."

She paused for a moment, fingered her wineglass, took a sip, and then added: "And, of course, as everyone knows, the better wines come from grapes that have been made to suffer."

I was not about to dispute her theories because I do not know all that much about plants and trees and the creatures that attack them. But I could not help relating what she said to how overly reliant we have become on artificial ways of preventing unwanted things from happening to us—that were we left alone we might solve ourselves and thereby be strengthened.

◆

Bum Knee

This has been a bad year; we have had only half our normal rainfall. That means that so far I have had to haul in four tons of alfalfa more than I ordinarily do because I cannot take the sheep out to graze as much as I do in other years.

Several months ago I drove the fifty miles over to Soledad to get another ton of hay, and in the process of loading it by hand, my left foot slipped through a gap between two bales and I wrenched my left knee. It was momentarily painful, but not enough to concern me at the time. It seemed no more than the usual aches and pains that go with doing farm work. Generally, one walks such injuries off, and in time the pain goes away and you are as good as new. But after a couple of weeks the pain got worse; my knee swelled up.

I did not go to my family physician because I figured he would send me to a specialist to make a final diagnosis anyway, so I went to a local orthopedist.

He made his examination and said I probably had torn the cartilage, which, he explained, does not heal as does other tissue of the body because there is no blood supply to it. The usual procedure is to insert an orthoscope and correct the problem, otherwise the torn tissue will act like grains of sand and irritate the inner surface of the kneecap. "It's a very simple procedure and is done on an outpatient basis. You'll be up and around the next day," he said. "We better have it X-rayed, though, to make sure you've torn a cartilage," he added.

Even though this reminded me of the time I took my injured lamb to the vet, I figured I better do as he said.

When I called for the results I was told that the doctor was out of town for the next couple of days, but that he had left a message for me to set up a date for surgery. I said I would let them know, for I had a number of things I needed to do first before I could arrange a definite time.

Over the weekend my daughter called to wish me a happy birthday, and in discussing my knee she said she knew a ballet dancer who also tore up her knee. Her orthopedist had recommended orthoscopic surgery, but she went to a sports orthopedist for a second opinion who recommended certain strengthening exercises instead of surgery. According to my daughter, the girl was back dancing in six weeks.

The next day I went to my regular family doctor, told him the X-rays had revealed a "tear in the posterior third of the medial meniscus," and sought a second opinion from him.

He examined my knee, twisting my ankle this way and that, asking if this or that hurt. Then he said, "If you were a quarterback earning a million a year and needed to play in another six weeks, I'd say yes to surgery. But for a man your age, why don't you try some strengthening exercises first and see what happens. In a couple of months, if it doesn't improve, you can always have surgery."

This reasoning rather appealed to me because when I was a kid at Hillside School I fell off a truck and injured my right ankle. I figured it was a sprain and hobbled around for a few weeks until the pain went away and everything seemed all right again.

Years later, when I was in the infantry and sprained the same ankle again, the army doctor asked if I had ever broken my ankle. I said I remembered spraining my ankle when I was around eleven years old.

"Well, the X-rays show you broke your malleolus back then."

"I did? I thought it was just a sprained ankle."

"It shows here a definite break." He looked at the X-rays again and then added, "All I can say is, you're a very lucky man. The treatment of choice then would have been for you to have your ankle in a cast. If they had immobilized your ankle it would have mended, but chances are you'd've had a limp for the rest of your life, hobbling around on a stiff ankle."

"What d'you mean lucky?" I scoffed. "If I had a stiff ankle they wouldn't've taken me in the army."

He laughed.

FALSE SPRING

The weather is surprising here. Sometimes in early spring, when I am still a shepherd and Maxie and I take the sheep out to graze on the green grass that will turn brown in a few weeks, the temperature turns warm. It is like summer and all of a sudden the insect world comes alive.

We stand on the observatory hill, and when I look toward the distant mountains and, thus, focus my eyes toward infinity, the atmosphere is alive with waves of invisible things, sensed more than seen. But when I focus my eyes for a closer look at the pond below, I see the air filled with unseen wings supporting needlelike bodies, some blue, some red, darting at, and in and around one another in a wild aerial dance celebrating a false spring. They do not know that in another day or so it will turn cold again and they must die. But for today, at least, they are alive and compelled by an urge to ensure that their kind will live beyond them and not know the reason why.

Perhaps primitive man, privileged at times like this to catch a glimpse of worlds beyond his knowing, considered the place where he experiences flashes of spiritual insight to be a holy place.

Humanity has always yearned to understand the world in which it lives. Even more intriguing are the worlds we perceive to lie hidden beyond it. But the truth sought in both worlds is often illusive, the face of God unseen. Yet we keep searching. If we were to give up that search mankind would be lost. Some seek it in the heavens—"out there" in outer space—whereas others seek a glimpse of the Unseen within themselves, contemplating it in lonely and cloistered cells, in prayer, in meditation, staring at the sun, or in books where the voices of past believers can be heard pondering the same imponderables of our existence that concern us today. Others are content to commune with nature and seek answers there.

Even so, some become impatient with conventional methods of inquiry and experimentally ingest substances that promise to alter the chemistry of their minds and transport them into uncharted worlds where they hope truth will, at last, be revealed in greater clarity, often to find oblivion a substitute for what they seek. They become lost in dreams and drop out because the dream of the reality is better for them than the reality of the dream. To each his own.

Perhaps having had a childhood handicap causes me to meet, even invite challenges in order to satisfy some need to prove to myself I am able to surmount any obstacle without having to rely on outside help. Perhaps it is a form of pride. Whatever.

Anyway, sometimes at night, when the sky is overcast and there are no stars to light up the sky, Maxie and I walk along the road that traverses the top of our mountain. I cannot see the ground. It is a challenge to walk under such a handicap, but I have found that if I look up at the treetops that line each side of the road, I can sense more than see a mirrored pathway in the sky to guide me. The paved road underneath my feet I can also feel; and if for a moment I step onto the soft shoulder of earth on either side I can then step back onto the paved surface, knowing that as long as I remain on it I will come to no harm. I feel as a blind man must feel. I use senses I ordinarily do not need but I know are always there when I need them.

This is not to say that the temptation to use means other than natural for finding excitement (or whatever else it is most of us seek) has not always been there for me and my generation.

♦

A Lie to Live By

Back before the Second World War, especially in the entertainment world when I was breaking into it, some of the musicians smoked a kind of roll-your-own cigarette they called a "reefer." (It is now called a joint, a substance more commonly referred to as pot or weed.) Smoking it was probably more prevalent in the musical profession than in others at the time. Its use was not widespread but we knew it was available, and it was offered with the zeal of those who wish to convert the uninitiated. We were told by them that it was harmless. Those who believed them tried it.

Now a promised thrill is always a temptation for the young, especially if he wants to be accepted as a regular guy, someone who will take a risk, a dare. Cocaine was also used. There was, of course, the hard stuff. (It was called smack.) We knew that once you got on to that you might as well give up because you were hooked for life; it became a very expensive habit; it also caused death if you overdosed. Therefore, we who had any sense at all avoided it. We were also told—and we believed it because there was plenty of evidence to support it—that the use of pot led to the use of cocaine, which led to the use of the ultimate and inevitable step, heroin.

Years later, when many of our young people found that marijuana was not as harmful as we had told them it was, they gave this as a reason (or an excuse) for doubting our generation's credibility on many other things. We may have been carriers of false information in this instance, but, fortunately, our ignorance saved us. It probably saved our whole generation from substituting pot for alcohol when the sale of alcohol was prohibited by law.

Yes, temptation is there for every generation, but my generation was lucky to have had a lie to live by.

♦

Writing for the Nonreader

When the air is warmer at our elevation than in the valley a temperature inversion occurs, causing the valley below to become filled with fog. The warmth above the fog forms a cap to keep it from evaporating into clouds to drift away to sea, or inland to drop rain to the east.

Several years ago I was walking toward the setting sun along the road that tops our ridge. The valley below was filled with fog. The surrounding mountains formed islands that poked up through it. When I turned around and headed for home, I faced a full moon just rising as the sun was setting behind me. I did not have the sheep with me and I hurried home, hoping to get there in time for me to share it with Louise. By the time I got home, however, the sun had already set and the horizon-enlarged moon had risen too high to dominate the east as it had only a few minutes before. The sun had sunk from view, but the moon, only recently flushed a deep dull red, was rapidly bleeding to death before my eyes, turning into a faded and wispy gray ghost, destined to wither away each succeeding night.

This concurrence of sun, moon, and fog has never repeated itself since then that I know of. I know it will someday if I live that long. It does come close at times, but the moon is never quite full enough, or it is a little late or too early for it to rise just as the sun is setting.

It is conceivable, of course, that one morning, when the fog fills the valley, I will awaken and witness the moon setting just as the sun is rising. At my age I find the rising sun a more appealing symbol than the one at the other end of the day. But whether the phenomenon I just described occurs at sunrise or sunset makes little difference to me as long as I can share it with Louise. I find as we come to the close of our lives that the things we value—it can be something as transient as a sunset, the moon rising, as brief as a thought, or a feeling of joy—I want to share it with her.

Writing a book is rather like that. It too is a sharing of experience. For me, probably because it was so difficult for me to master, the written word has always been important. The images words are able to evoke in my imagination are sometimes more compelling and exciting than the real thing. Think, therefore, if you will, what those who cannot read are missing.

I suppose, in a way, you could say that it is for the nonreader that this book was written or, at least, dedicated. Now I know that is right up there with painting pictures for the blind and composing music for the deaf, but I recently read that in America at least one person in five cannot read. That is twenty percent of our whole population! I figure that is well over forty million people who are functionally illiterate. Other estimates are more conservative, claiming the number to be anywhere from one to ten million. Still, that is a lot of folks who cannot read to have written a book for.

Back when I felt I was the only one in the whole world who could not read, I tried to hide it from others. I became a great faker. I played all sorts of deceptive games to keep others from knowing. I knew I was fooling no one but myself, but this handicap made me feel I would be less well thought of if I was ever found out. Consequently, I erected all sorts of defenses that warped my personality in other ways, and it has taken me a lifetime to overcome them. I am still working on it. And I suppose, if drugs were as readily available in grade school then as apparently they are now, I might easily have slipped into using them, as so many of our young people do today, especially those who have a handicap similar to the one I had. They say that eighty percent of the inmates in prison are functionally illiterate. At one time when I was separated from my mother I could easily have developed a permanent criminal attitude.

THE EFFICACY OF FAITH

It is time I came clean and admitted some facts about myself that I have withheld until now. A lot happened to me during the war. After Pearl Harbor, when we were actually doing battle with an enemy and all the isolationists had turned quiet and I saw I was "in for the duration," I figured I better do something about it: I went to OCS and became an infantry officer. Later (for the "convenience of the government," it was called), I transferred in grade and became a pilot and ended up as a flight leader flying combat with

When I was growing up, a person who could n could still get by. He could become a farmer, a cow laborer, even an operator of machines (or a hou seamstress, factory worker, or a domestic) and coul enough to support a family. In today's high-tech s however, it is much more important for a worker to b to read. As more and more factories become mecha with robots, replacing skilled workers who once di need to read to do their jobs, it becomes necessary fc rest of us to support those who cannot. Moreover, person who has no other thing going for him than h cundity, in which his or her self-regard is enhanced on an ability to propagate, it can only add to an evergro population of underprivileged children, who, the exp tell us, are likely to have children who will also hav reading disability. Whether this is genetically, socially, n ally or economically caused is not for me to say; that is the experts to decide.

the Chinese Air Force under Chennault.

But that is a story for another time.

Four years later, after the war was over, I did not go back into show business. I had to make a living in order to support a family. Therefore I became a businessman for about six or seven years. But then I got religion, went to seminary and was ordained an Episcopal priest. I was in the active ministry for some years, during which time I was a civil rights activist. But that too is a story for another time.

Then, I went back to school, got my doctorate and became a clinical psychologist, which I remained until I retired and became a rancher.

Admitting all this at this time, and thus blowing my cover, allows me to bring this book to a close on what I consider a proper note.

I was counseling a couple whose marriage was in the process of breaking up. They asked me to see their daughter. They were concerned that their marital problems were filtering down to her. They were. But incidental to that, or because of it, she had numerous warts on her hands. She told me that none of the doctors she had gone to could rid her of them. Warts were not her present problem, of course, but I told her how my grandmother got rid of my warts back when I was a kid.

♦

Warts and All

I had done none of the things one supposedly does to cause a wart—like the myth about handling toads—but there one was on the knuckle of my little finger. It seemed to have appeared overnight. I somehow knew my grandmother would know what to do about it. Not only did she know about things like warts, but she was a great one for telling stories. She loved stories. So did I. We would sit with the lights out in front of the fireplace and she would tell ghost stories. She knew a lot about how boys thought, of course, having had three of her own.

"Do you really want to get rid of it?" she asked, knowing I might like having the wart because I was probably the only boy in the neighborhood who did.

After I hesitated a moment, I said, "Yes." I was interested in how she would go about getting rid of it. When you are the age I was you never know when information like that can be helpful in case you have to handle a whole bunch of toads.

Now she did not go into some weird kind of trance or anything like that, but all of a sudden a mysterious change came over her, as though she were letting me know that something important was about to happen and she was letting me in on it. She went to the icebox and got out a slab of bacon, cut off a tiny piece, came back and, in dignified solemnity, she rubbed the bacon on the wart.

She then whispered in that spooky way of hers: "Now you bury this somewhere no one will find it, and in about a week, after it's had time to molder in the ground, the wart will disappear.

"But it won't work," she warned, "unless you're nice to everyone, especially the ones you don't get on with." (She was always throwing in things like that to make it my responsibility if it did not work. I suppose it got her off the hook if her magic failed, allowing her to retain her credibility, like all faith healers tend to do.)

I did as she said and, behold, in about a week the wart was gone, just as she had promised.

I have since learned that warts are caused by a virus. The chemistry in our bodies wards the viruses off except in times of stress when our immune systems can no longer keep them from erupting in the form of cold sores and warts.

There are, undoubtedly, other factors involved that science has been unable to determine as to what causes such phenomena; but as far as my grandmother and I were concerned, we had something that science is also unable to measure, such as the healing powers of trust and persuasion. Some people call it faith.

After I told the young lady about my grandmother's cure for warts, she looked at me with amused skepticism. "Why not?" she said with a shrug, "I've tried everything else."

I wish I could say her warts disappeared in a week as mine had when my grandmother had worked her magic on me. I believe the reason they did not is that she did not have the same faith in my grandmother's cure as I had. Nor did she have faith in me, her other doctors, or anybody else, for that matter. At least, that is my explanation, for I have since concluded that some people do not ever want to be cured of what ails them. They say they do; they may even believe they do, but they resist change. They want to remain the same, warts and all. They lack faith. They have lost hope that it is, indeed, within their power to allow change to take place.

To give an example of what I mean: Some years ago I saw an emotionally disturbed woman in the hospital. She was in a deep depression, cause unknown. During our initial session she asked to see a clergyman. Although I was ordained, I felt it was more appropriate for her to see the hospital chaplain. I was functioning as her therapist and did not want her to confuse the two roles. I was afraid she might, as some patients do, have a negative stereotype about clergymen being straightlaced and overly judgmental (some are), causing her to withhold helpful information about herself she considered too offensive to be heard by a man of the cloth.

The next day she returned and said the chaplain had told her that I, too, was a clergyman. I admitted that I was. "Then you can give me absolution," she said.

I said I could, considering this a rare opportunity that is not always offered in therapy so soon. I saw that she trusted me and, based on that trust, knew she would now be more likely to open up and tell me what had triggered her depression. I asked her what "sin" she wanted to confess and have God forgive.

She said she had used abusive language ("Swear words," she said) toward members of her family while in a fit of anger.

When she did not elaborate, I asked, "Is that all?"

"Yes."

"Is there anything more you want to tell?"

"No."

Some confession, I thought. But I also knew that sometimes the most seemingly inconsequential thing can take on enormous importance to those who must find a reason—

any reason—that seems plausible enough to give them justification for feeling as miserable as they do.

I told her to kneel. She did. I rose and gave her absolution.

I had spoken the words hundreds of times before. I must confess it was in more formal situations than this. But I have never experienced so dramatic a result before or since. At that very moment this woman's depression lifted.

You can say she was crazy. She was. And despite her sudden and astounding recovery, I knew her psychosis was still there in the chemistry of her mind and body. But I also know that just as the news of the death of a loved one can stun us into the throes of grief, so too can good news cause a chemical flood of euphoria to engulf us.

There is another way of putting it: She had faith in the efficacy of the words of absolution as I had in my grandmother's cure for warts. I had merely brought her the Good News, as my grandmother had brought me. Chemistry, or whatever, took over from there, allowing the body to heal itself.

AFTERWORD: WHAT'S IN A NAME?

All the while I was writing this book I had a working title. I thought *Thoughts While Tending Sheep* was a good descriptive title.

"But you've got to get a better title than that," I was told. "You've got to think of a more catchy title, one that will make people want to read it."

I spent the whole next week trying to think of a better one. A couple came to mind: *They Say Sheep Are Dumb* was one. The other was *And Every Shepherd Tells His Tale*, quoting Milton's "L'Allegro." Neither satisfied me. Louise was as helpful as she usually is when it comes to names. *Thoughts You Can Ewes* was her first suggestion, followed by, *Ewesful Reflections.* These were made without comment. She felt the following needed an explanation, however. She said: "In order to attract the Yuppy, high-tech computer crowd, how about *Ewes 'R Friendly?*"

Her suggestions helped put it all in perspective. I decided then and there I would stick with the original—unless, of course, the publishing of this book is dependent on a title change. I can see nothing wrong with a title that can be appropriately followed by another in a series. For instance, I could entitle the next one, *More Thoughts While Tending Sheep*, followed by another with the title of *Still More Thoughts While Tending Sheep.*

The possibilities are endless, especially if I had to give up the sheep business because of marauding lions, the rising cost of alfalfa, my bum knee, or the aging process. I could always start the next book with the title *Second Thoughts About Tending Sheep*, or even *Thoughts While Not Tending Sheep*, and so on. We will see.

ACKNOWLEDGMENTS

I am grateful to Jim and Anne Pritchard, Mary Page, Betty Wilson, Jim Brock, and Bill Webb for their suggested changes to the completed manuscript just prior to its being submitted for publication.

I also wish to thank members of the Published Writers Group, a local group of writers who meet once a week and criticize (Criticize? Do we ever!) one another's efforts. It consists of Tom Ainsworth, M.D., Tom and Joan Condon, Jim Greenan, Mary Krainik, Beverly Paik, Helen Parker, Tony Seton, and Evelyn Smart. Great writers all. Also thanks to my sister, Georgiana, who read the manuscript to check our family history, etc., for accuracy.

Also, there is James O'Shea Wade, my editor, whose good taste, knowledge, patience, and tact with an "about-to-be-published writer," made the effort all worthwhile.

And, of course, there is Louise; without a lifetime of her love and encouragement I could not have made it.